TAKE BACK YOUR BRAIN

TAKE BACK YOUR BRAIN

Reclaiming Your Power
with Brain-Centered Living

ILCHI LEE

952 E Baseline Rd. Suite 101
Gilbert, AZ 85204
www.BestLifeMedia.com
480-926-2480

First paperback edition: March 2025
Library of Congress Control Number: 2025930366
ISBN-13: 978-1-947502-33-8

Cover and interior design by Kiryl Lysenka

*To all who believe in the power
of their minds and hearts.*

CONTENTS

Contents

AUTHOR'S NOTE

IT'S TIME TO TAKE BACK YOUR BRAIN

Our brains hold the key to achieving everything we aspire to in life. They power our ability to think, feel, dream, and create—making them the most extraordinary tool we possess. Yet, in today's world, we often lose control of this precious resource, surrendering it to distractions and influences that limit its true potential.

Take smartphones, for example. They promise connection and convenience, but the more we use them, the more isolated, distracted, and disconnected we become. Technology meant to unite us now constantly overwhelms our attention. With nonstop exposure to fragmented, overstimulating content, our brains are losing the ability to think deeply and connect meaningfully.

Social media isn't much different. What was once a way to share small moments of joy has become a source of comparison, anxiety, and conflict. Instead of inspiring us, seeing others' success and happiness often makes us feel inadequate. A space designed for open discussion has shifted to one that highlights differences and fuels division. The more time we spend on it, the more our brains get hooked, leaving us unbalanced, anxious, and biased.

Through smartphones and social media, we are constantly exposed to ads that play on our insecurities, telling us we need to fix ourselves to feel happy. The drive to "have more" and "be happier" traps us in endless consumption. Yet, this pursuit of material gain provides only temporary satisfaction and never leads to lasting happiness. Over time, our brains get stuck in a cycle of craving instant gratification and constantly chasing the next thing.

Schools and society are supposed to nurture our imagination and creativity, but often they do the opposite. We're taught to prioritize correct answers, avoid mistakes, and follow the safest path. Eventually, we lose the freedom to dream and challenge ourselves, focusing instead on chasing high salaries, stable jobs, and prestigious degrees. Caught up in meeting society's expectations and playing it safe, our minds become rigid. We lose curiosity, flexibility, and the ability to listen to our inner voice.

The biggest threat to our brains isn't just what comes from the outside—it's what happens inside. Negative thinking, self-doubt, and limiting beliefs often have a stronger hold than external influences. When past failures, bad experiences, or fears about things that haven't even happened take over, it becomes hard to imagine a better future. Thoughts like, "I'm not good enough," "I can't do this," or "This is too much for me" grow stronger the more we repeat them, creating even greater barriers to moving forward.

The constant flow of information we consume profoundly affects how we think, feel, and act. Gradually, we become so used to certain types of content that we can even become addicted to it. As we rely more and more on content filtered by AI algorithms that feed our addictions, we lose our ability to make decisions and judgments for ourselves. Instead of being creative and proactive, our brains become passive, simply reacting to whatever comes our way.

About This Book

We need to take back our brains. This means reclaiming them from the overwhelming flood of unmindful information, the digital devices that dominate our attention, and the stereotypes and habits that hold us back. Taking back our brains is about regaining control over how we process and evaluate information, reestablishing the brain as the center of creation and guidance in our lives—not just a passive reactor to external influences.

At the heart of this journey is the concept of the BrainPhone. Imagine a natural capacity within you, more powerful than any smartphone, that connects you to your inner wisdom, creativity, and intuition. The BrainPhone symbolizes the limitless potential of your brain. Turning it on means shifting your focus inward, tapping into the mind's ability to create, intuit, and bring your deepest goals to life. This is the first step in reclaiming your brain and becoming the true master of your thoughts and actions.

To turn on your BrainPhone, I recommend engaging in activities that align your mind, body, and spirit—what I call Brain Sports. These are not just sets of exercises but a lifestyle—a way of living that transforms everyday activities into opportunities for growth and development. This includes physical practices like pull-ups, mental practices like meditation, and creative pursuits like imagination. Simply put, Brain Sports are the tools to activate your BrainPhone and awaken your brain's full potential.

This book offers practical guidance on activating your BrainPhone and integrating Brain Sports into your daily routine. You'll learn how to connect with your inner feelings, break free from limiting beliefs, and use imagination and creativity to align your actions with your goals. Step-by-step suggestions and real-life examples will show you how to bring balance, joy, and fulfillment into your life.

In the final chapters, I explore what I believe to be the highest potential of the human brain: its divinity. By recognizing and embracing this capacity, we can unlock new opportunities for personal growth and contribute to positive change in the world.

The Sage's Mind

When we awaken the divinity within our brain, it unlocks creativity, conscience, empathy, and a genuine desire to improve the world. When these qualities are active, we can use the brain's incredible power to help others, not just ourselves. I call this quality the "sage's mind," and I believe it holds the hope for humanity.

Many consider sages to be morally perfect beings or great spiritual teachers like Jesus, Buddha, Confucius, or Muhammad. This makes the thought of being a sage feel irrelevant to our lives or like something reserved for extraordinary people. The thought that "I can be a sage" often gets dismissed as arrogant or unrealistic, but this comes from misunderstanding what a sage truly is.

The sages we need today are not perfect individuals or people with extraordinary powers. They are those who reveal the divine within themselves and live out their love and responsibility—for themselves, for others, and for the world. Our planet needs not only one or two sages but millions of them.

Every day, we face severe global crises, including climate change, war, violence, and political conflict. These problems cannot be solved unless we all work together. In today's interconnected world, even the most minor actions by ordinary people can create meaningful change on a global level.

Many people are already stepping up because they care about others and the planet. This sense of responsibility and care for the world is the heart of the sage's mind. We all have this within us. Anyone can make this part of themselves more visible and active—it just takes awareness, courage, and practice.

Our brain's abilities are too precious to waste. The planet we live on is too rare in the universe to let it be destroyed. Humanity holds too much potential to give up. And this moment in history is a unique opportunity that we may never get again if we fail to act.

We have a brain, and we have a mind that guides it. Within both lie the answers we seek and the future we hope for. When we consciously choose to use our brains with intention, we can create healthier, happier, and more meaningful lives. If we decide to use our brains for peace and coexistence instead of competition and destruction, we can make a better future for everyone.

I hope this book helps you take back your brain and make choices that benefit both your life and the world around you.

Ilchi Lee

CHAPTER 1

WHEN MACHINES STEAL OUR MINDS

What's one thing most of us carry everywhere and can't imagine living without? For many, it's their smartphone. Think about the last time you forgot your phone at home—how did it feel? We've all experienced that uneasy, disoriented day, fumbling through tasks without it. From checking emails to managing schedules or staying connected with friends, it's become nearly impossible to function without this little device.

The thought of losing your smartphone is enough to spark panic. You go to call a friend but realize you don't know their number by heart. Your phone holds everything—photos, videos, personal information, and even your banking apps—and the idea of someone else getting access to it is terrifying. Research shows just how stressful this can be. A 2017 survey by the Physiological Society in the UK found that losing a smartphone is nearly as stressful as facing a terrorist threat.

Smartphones have only been widely used for about 20 years, but they've completely changed our lives. They're not just phones anymore; they're cameras, calculators, maps, recorders, radios, TVs, and miniature computers. We use them for work, school, entertainment, and almost everything else. We once relied on libraries or friends to answer questions, but today, the world fits in our pockets, accessible with just a swipe.

Smartphones Don't Make Us Smart

We rely on our smartphones every day, but are they making our lives smarter? Or are they making us more distracted and less focused? They're certainly not helping our health. Most of us have felt the stiff neck, dry eyes, and foggy head that results from staring at a screen for too long. Many people have trouble sleeping because they stay up late, scrolling on their phones. But the more serious issue is how dependent we've become on them mentally.

Smartphones have turned into a constant distraction. We check them out of habit—while working, eating, or even when spending time with someone we care about. Notifications and endless scrolling pull us away from the present moment. With all that constant scrolling, we're processing so much information so quickly that we end up jumping from one thing to the next, like a grasshopper. No wonder it's getting harder to focus on anything for so long.

A 2023 study by Gloria Mark at the University of California, Irvine, found that most of us cannot focus on a screen for more than 47 seconds. Compare that to 20 years ago, when people could focus for two and a half minutes. We're also losing the chance to strengthen our memory. There was a time when we memorized phone numbers and found our way around without GPS using maps, our memories, or directions given by a friend. Now, many of us rely on our phones, even to check our own home addresses.

Oxford University Press in the UK chose "brain rot" as its word of the year for 2024. It describes the mental decline that happens when we spend too much time on mindless social media content. Researchers have confirmed that excessive screen time can indeed diminish cognition, noting that many young people are now displaying symptoms like early-stage dementia—poor memory, lack of focus, diminished social skills, and negligent self-care.

Furthermore, technology can dull our natural curiosity and creativity. In one fun experiment conducted by Loyola Marymount University professors, two groups of people were asked to design and fly paper airplanes, but one could access Google and the other could not. The Google group created the overall furthest-flying airplanes since they could get directions from paper plane enthusiasts all over the world. However, while the non-Internet group created a lot of failures, they also created the most innovative designs and two airplanes that flew farther than any in the Google group.

Most of us start our day by grabbing our phones as soon as we wake up and don't set them down until bedtime. The content on our phones is designed to keep us hooked. You might watch one video to unwind, but before you know it, hours have passed. Features like infinite scrolling, autoplay, and recommendations constantly nudge us with "Watch this!" or "You'll love this!" making it hard to stop. Some of us even check our phones in the shower or on the toilet. Later, when we can't access our phones, we feel anxious and unsettled, like we're going through withdrawal. Especially since the COVID-19 pandemic, which left many people with little to do beyond scrolling the Internet, pathological Internet addiction has increased exponentially.

Whenever we check our phones—whether for new messages, a like on social media, or an interesting post—our brains release dopamine. This chemical gives us a quick burst of pleasure, making us want to do it again. Over time, these small rewards build up, and we reach for our phones more often. This repeated behavior becomes a habit, making us more dependent on our smartphones. The process happens so unconsciously that most of us don't even notice how addicted we've become.

Smartphone addiction isn't just killing productivity—it's taking a serious toll on our mental health. Whether you're a kid or an adult, smartphones make us impatient. We've gotten used to instant communication through short videos or quick text replies, making us less tolerant. If we send a text and don't get an answer immediately, it's easy to feel annoyed or even angry. As this continues, we lose the ability to manage our emotions, and more people are finding it hard to handle feelings like anger or anxiety.

Smartphone dependency also changes how we interact with others. When family or friends get together, conversations remain shallow because everyone is glued to their phones. It's common for couples to lie in bed at night, each on their own phone, leaving little time to talk about their day or share what's on their mind.

For many teens, texting on a smartphone feels easier than having face-to-face conversations, even with close friends. Gradually, this makes in-person interactions feel awkward or even stressful, weakening their ability to empathize or connect emotionally with others.

Losing Touch with Who We Are

Of all the problems caused by smartphone dependency, what worries me most is how disconnected we've become from ourselves. The more time we spend connected to our devices, the less time we spend connecting with ourselves. When you're on your smartphone, you're constantly hit with notifications, emails, news, and social media, all competing for your attention. Over time, you get used to focusing outward instead of inward. You work all day, come home, and pick up your phone again to unwind. There's little time or energy left to reflect or connect with yourself. We're so busy consuming external content that we forget to listen to our inner voice.

But real happiness and fulfillment come from staying connected to yourself. You can't fully understand your emotions, feelings, or what you truly want if you don't take the time to reflect. When you're always caught up in outside distractions, you lose touch with who you are and what really matters to you. Spending every spare moment on your phone leaves little time to pause and reflect. Instead, short, flashy content takes over your mind, leaving you further disconnected.

We're perpetually comparing ourselves to others through our smartphones. Seeing other people's fancy houses, perfect bodies, or amazing vacations can make our own lives feel small and unworthy. Even when we know this content is curated and often far from reality, it's hard to avoid doubting ourselves, feeling inferior, and questioning our self-worth.

This cycle of comparison changes how we see ourselves. Instead of focusing on our own values and goals, we start relying on external validation to feel good about who we are. Bit by bit, we lose touch with our inner sense of worth and begin measuring it against an endless stream of filtered, idealized images.

In his book *The Anxious Generation*, Jonathan Haidt points out that Generation Z—those born in and after 1996—is facing a severe mental health crisis. The statistics he presented are shocking. Between 2010 and 2020, the rate of self-harm among American Gen Z girls almost tripled, and the suicide rate rose by about 2.5 times. Haidt asks, "What happened to our young people in the early 2010s?"

His analysis examines the rise of smartphones and social media, which shifted kids' lives from a "play-based childhood" to a "phone-based childhood." Before smartphones, children spent time outside playing, moving, learning to solve conflicts, reading social cues, and managing their emotions.

Now, as smartphones and social media dominate their lives, face-to-face interactions have dropped dramatically, and unsupervised outdoor free play has nearly disappeared. At the same time, overprotective parenting has taken away many opportunities for kids to take risks, challenge themselves, and build resilience. As a result, Gen Z is dealing with social disconnection, sleep deprivation, poor concentration, and smartphone addiction.

A few years ago, a leaked internal Facebook document revealed that Instagram was making anxiety and depression worse for teens. The report showed shocking numbers: 13 percent of teens in the UK and 6 percent in the US said they had suicidal thoughts while using Instagram. In my home country, South Korea, the issue is just as serious, with more teens dying from suicide than from accidents or illness.

It's heartbreaking to see so many young people struggling with self-loathing and thoughts of suicide. I know what that feels like. When I was in school, I often felt like I had nothing to offer the world. I remember looking at the trash piled under a bridge near my home and thinking I was just as insignificant and useless as that garbage. My life started to change when I realized I wasn't worthless and that I could help others and make a difference.

Over the past 45 years, I've worked with so many people on their personal growth, and one thing has become clear to me: the foundation of a happy, successful life is knowing your self-worth and respecting yourself. To do that, you have to connect with yourself. But the digital world we live in today makes that harder than ever, cutting us off from something so essential to our well-being.

Reclaiming Our Minds

Digital devices like smartphones have become our go-to tools for accessing information. They let us consume content faster and more conveniently than ever. But how often do we actually choose what we're taking in, process it carefully, and respond with our own judgment?

In today's constant stream of information, much of what enters our minds does so without our even realizing it. Yet, this information profoundly influences us. It affects how we think, feel, and act. Repeated exposure to the same types of content doesn't just form habits—it can change how we see ourselves and the world.

Take this example: if we're regularly exposed to stories about crime, violence, and conflict, it's natural to start believing that "the world is a dangerous place." This belief can subtly shape how we interact with others. Instead of approaching people in our lives with openness, we may become cautious or even distrustful, especially of those who seem different from us. Of course, there are times to be cautious around people we don't know or in unfamiliar circumstances. However, questions like, "Could this person harm me?" start to influence how we view everyone, not just strangers.

This defensive mindset can make us more guarded and heighten our competitiveness in unhealthy ways. We might begin to think, "If the world is so unsafe, I need to be stronger to survive," causing us to focus more on outpacing others than on working together. Over time, this outlook shifts our emotions, too. Feelings like fear and anxiety start to dominate, making it harder to experience hope, optimism, or joy. Instead of seeing possibilities and connections, we get stuck in a cycle of worry and mistrust.

As technology evolves, the way we receive information becomes more automated and sophisticated. The AI algorithms in our smartphones track what we like and how we behave to keep us engaged for as long as possible.

At first, these algorithms feel like helpful tools, showing us content we enjoy. But before we even realize it, we start to depend on them. Instead of guiding our choices, they begin to shape them. While we scroll through our feeds, our brains shift into autopilot, passively absorbing what's presented. In exchange for convenience, we're giving up our ability to think critically and make our own decisions.

Navigation apps are a perfect example. They're incredibly useful, but many of us feel lost—literally and figuratively—when we don't have one to guide us. This reliance on technology becomes a habit, and we stop exercising our own problem-solving skills. If this continues, we risk losing our confidence in making decisions without the help of AI. This isn't just about individual habits. It's a broader issue that challenges the incredible potential of the human brain to think, create, and choose freely.

I'm not saying we should stop using smartphones or other high-tech devices. They've become essential to modern life. These tools are so integrated into our daily routines that, without them, we often feel stuck or even helpless. The key is not rejecting technology but cultivating practices that help us reclaim our minds, connect with ourselves, and tap into our potential.

As smartphones and artificial intelligence develop further, they'll handle tasks faster and more efficiently than we ever could. But no matter how advanced these tools become, they won't solve deeper issues like the need to find happiness, improve our relationships, or address global challenges like climate change or inequality. New technology and systems are important, but they're not enough to fix humanity's problems at their root.

At the center of all this is our mind. It guides our choices and shapes how we use the technology and resources we've created.

These tools can either drain our energy and divide us, or they can empower us and bring us closer together. The direction we choose will depend on our individual values and the collective mindset of our communities, which in turn depend on the content of our minds and hearts.

As we rely more on smartphones and external conveniences, the risk of losing touch with ourselves grows. Yet, the power to reclaim our minds is always within reach. The first step is choosing to take back control—not from technology itself, but from the habits and culture that pull us away from who we truly are.

CHAPTER 2

TURN ON YOUR BRAINPHONE

Every day, we rely on our brains to solve problems, make decisions, and navigate life's challenges. Yet, we often take its remarkable abilities for granted. Our brains are nothing short of a miracle—an extraordinary tool that enables us to learn, adapt, and create, shaping both our lives and the world.

Think about humanity's once-unimaginable technologies such as electricity, airplanes, and smartphones. These breakthroughs didn't happen by chance—they came from human brains thinking creatively, solving problems, and persisting in the face of challenges. The same is true for transformative social changes, like advancing equality and protecting the environment. At its best, the brain is a powerful guide for progress and a miracle-maker.

But this power isn't limited to historical achievements—it extends to each of us. Every time you learn a new skill, overcome a setback, or adapt to a challenge, your brain forms new connections and helps you grow. Scientists call this neuroplasticity—the brain's ability to change and develop throughout your life. Whether mastering a new recipe, navigating a tough situation, or fostering a meaningful connection with someone you care about, your brain is constantly improving and evolving.

What makes this possible is the interplay between your brain and your mind. The mind is the conscious part of you that observes, reflects, and decides. It's what allows you to pause, think, and choose how to respond to challenges. This ability to reflect and adapt elevates the brain from remarkable to truly miraculous.

Yet in today's fast-paced, distraction-filled world, it's easy to lose touch with this power. We spend so much time reacting to external demands that we rarely pause to focus inward, where real transformation happens. To take back our brains and unlock their full potential, we must intentionally shift our attention—away from the noise of the outside world and toward the mind within.

The BrainPhone, Your Brain's Expansive Mode

I have always believed in the immense power of the human mind to improve our lives and create a better future for the world. This belief has guided my journey to study the mind, explore its potential, and teach others how to tap into its power. Along the way, I became deeply fascinated by the brain as the physical foundation of the mind and sought practical ways to harness its capabilities effectively.

The brain is guided by the mind, which drives us to understand ourselves and shape the kind of life and world we want.

Engaging the brain isn't just about retaining information or storing knowledge—it's about awakening the mind and using it to create real change. When we understand how the brain and the mind work together, we uncover our ability to transform our reality.

To illustrate this relationship, I often reference the smartphones we use daily. We marvel at their features, spend hours exploring their functions, and depend on them for information and connection. Yet, how often do we devote that same level of attention to understanding and developing our brains? Imagine what we could achieve if we invested even a fraction of that energy into unlocking our brain's potential.

This reflection inspired the concept of the BrainPhone. The BrainPhone is a natural system within the brain that connects us to its limitless possibilities. Much like a smartphone connects us to the world, the BrainPhone links us to our inner resources, such as intuition, creativity, and insight. Unlike a physical device, the BrainPhone is not something external or artificial—it's a capability we are all born with and can activate intentionally.

The BrainPhone is already at work, influencing your life whether you realize it or not. However, by consciously activating it, you can fully harness its potential. I call this process "turning it on." Simply put, turning on your BrainPhone means shifting your focus inward, quieting distractions, and using your brain with intention. It's the first step toward taking control and unlocking more of your brain's capabilities.

Most of the time, we operate in what I call the brain's "default mode," where we react automatically to our environment. This mode helps us manage everyday tasks, but it limits our ability to see the bigger picture or access deeper insights. Turning on your BrainPhone takes you out of this reactive state and into a more conscious, intentional mode of operation. It's like saying to yourself, "I'm in charge of my brain, and I'm going to use it to create a better life."

When you activate your BrainPhone, your brain shifts from default mode to what I call "expansive mode." This shift is like upgrading from a flashlight to a searchlight—it allows you to see more clearly, recognize new possibilities, and make choices that align with your deeper values and goals.

Expansive mode goes beyond achieving clarity; it unlocks the brain's ability to think creatively, solve complex problems, and connect with a greater sense of purpose. In this state, the brain isn't just reacting to circumstances; it becomes a tool for intentional living, guiding you toward meaningful actions and decisions.

I also refer to this expansive mode as the brain's "spiritual mode" because it connects us to something greater than ourselves. In this mode, the brain quiets the noise of external distractions and taps into inner wisdom, universal truths, and a deeper sense of purpose. It's a state that fosters alignment with the flow of life, empowering us to live authentically and purposefully while remaining fully engaged with reality.

In spiritual mode, the BrainPhone helps us access clarity, balance, and fulfillment. It connects us with our true selves and allows us to live in harmony with our highest values. This connection empowers us to navigate life's challenges with grace and to build a life that reflects our deepest aspirations.

From Brain Rot to Brain Glory

To enter its expansive mode, the brain goes through a process of growth and development. In our daily lives, however, we may often find ourselves stuck in a state of "brain rot." This condition arises from the overwhelming demands of excessive information and constant stimulation. It manifests as mental exhaustion—where focus and creativity seem to evaporate, energy is depleted, and thoughts feel scattered. Negative emotions tend to take over, leaving your brain feeling sluggish and unproductive. But this state isn't permanent; it's a clear signal that your brain is crying out for renewal and care.

The good news is that you can reverse this process by activating your BrainPhone. This tool revitalizes your brain, taking it from a state of rot to one of blossom, radiance, and, ultimately, glory.

The journey begins by shifting your brain out of its sluggish state into a state of blossom. In this phase, your brain regains balance, energy flows more smoothly, emotions stabilize, and curiosity returns. Activating your BrainPhone unlocks these changes, laying a foundation for growth.

As your brain continues to develop, it moves from blossom to radiance. This phase is marked by enhanced imagination, creativity, and insight. With your BrainPhone fully engaged, your thoughts become clearer, and you gain the ability to set meaningful goals and take steps to achieve them. The brain becomes a powerful ally, supporting you in overcoming challenges and exploring your aspirations.

At its peak, the brain reaches a state of glory, where its full mental and spiritual potential is realized. Activating your

BrainPhone fosters alignment between your values and daily actions, leading to a profound sense of fulfillment. Gratitude, unconditional love, and a desire to contribute positively to the world define this stage, as the brain's inherent greatness shines through.

By turning on your BrainPhone, you guide your brain through the journey from blossom to radiance and ultimately to glory. Each step brings you closer to a richer, more purposeful life where the brain becomes a true partner in shaping your journey.

Smartphones vs. BrainPhones

Just as smartphones connect us to networks for communication and information, the BrainPhone connects us to an invisible network of inner knowledge and creative energy. Both are tools for connection—smartphones help us engage with the outside world, while the BrainPhone helps us tune into ourselves. By connecting inward, we can better understand our thoughts and feelings, gaining the clarity and focus needed to take purposeful action in our daily lives.

Smartphones come with apps to perform specific tasks like taking photos or tracking health metrics. Similarly, the BrainPhone has apps that correspond to the mind's potential. For example, the imagination app helps you push the boundaries of reality and explore endless possibilities. The intuition app uncovers solutions that logic alone might miss. A creativity app allows you to generate ideas that inspire meaningful change. Activating the BrainPhone allows you to tap into these apps and access your innate strengths.

Using your BrainPhone is as simple as opening an app on your smartphone, but instead of tapping a screen, you direct your attention inward. When you feel stressed, you can take a moment to breathe deeply and focus on your inner self rather than the source of your stress. Or you can ask yourself a meaningful question, such as, "What can I do to respond differently next time?" and reflect on the answer that emerges.

The main difference between a smartphone and a BrainPhone is what they connect us to. While smartphones connect us to external information, the BrainPhone provides access to inner clarity, resilience, and wisdom. Always accessible and self-sufficient, it requires no external power—only our focus and intention.

While smartphones are helpful, overuse can lead to dependency, stress, and disconnection from yourself. In contrast, the BrainPhone deepens your connection to your inner self. By setting aside your smartphone and turning on your BrainPhone, you shift your focus inward, rediscover your inner strength, and build the confidence to live with purpose and intention.

The Gifts of the BrainPhone

When we turn on our BrainPhones, we unlock many powerful gifts. One of the most valuable is self-discovery, where we reconnect with our true selves beyond the roles and labels imposed by society. This deeper connection helps us answer essential questions like, "Who am I?" "What do I truly want?" and "What is my place in the world?" It allows us to trust ourselves and make decisions with confidence, guided by an inner sense of what's right. Genuine self-understanding starts with getting to know yourself, and the BrainPhone's most important role is to help create that connection.

Another gift is improved problem-solving. Activating your BrainPhone sharpens intuition and insight, making it easier to uncover the root of a problem and discover meaningful solutions. Intuition helps you swiftly grasp the heart of an issue, directing your focus to what truly matters without the weight of overthinking or unnecessary details. Insight complements this by offering a broader perspective, helping you uncover underlying causes rather than just addressing surface-level symptoms. Together, they enable you to approach challenges with clarity and develop practical, effective solutions.

The BrainPhone also unlocks your creativity, helping you generate new ideas and turn them into meaningful action. By tapping into limitless imagination and fresh energy, it frees you from past limitations, opens new possibilities, and gives you the courage to bring them to life.

Finally, the BrainPhone enhances empathy by helping us better understand ourselves and others. When we become more aware of our own thoughts and emotions, it's easier to relate to the feelings and perspectives of those around us. This empathy strengthens relationships, reduces conflict, and improves communication, laying the foundation for a more compassionate and fulfilling life.

BrainPhone in Action

We've all experienced the power of the BrainPhone in our daily lives. Consider those moments when a solution to a problem suddenly appears after seeming elusive for so long. These "light bulb moments" or "flashes of inspiration" occur because your BrainPhone activates, tapping into your inner wisdom. It might happen while you're taking a shower, walking down the street, or recalling a conversation. These are clear examples of your BrainPhone at work.

The history of science and innovation also demonstrates the BrainPhone in action. Newton realized the law of gravity after observing an apple fall. Einstein relied on intuition to develop the theory of relativity. Mendeleev famously dreamed of the periodic table before formalizing it. These breakthroughs weren't random—they emerged from deeply engaging with a problem and allowing the brain to connect with its inner resources, uncovering insights beyond logic or analysis. Such moments highlight how activating the BrainPhone unlocks our innate wisdom and boundless creativity.

Decision-making provides another example. No matter how much we analyze the pros and cons or seek advice, the right choice sometimes remains unclear. Then, out of nowhere, clarity strikes—a deep sense of certainty and unwavering confidence arises, and we know exactly what to do. These moments of conviction are yet another way the BrainPhone manifests its power.

In my own life, my BrainPhone has guided me through pivotal moments. Today, hundreds of centers around the world teach the brain training methods I developed, but it all started with a simple decision. One morning, I listened to my inner voice urging me to share my experiences with others, so I went to a local park to take the first step.

My BrainPhone was also active when I sought ways to share traditional Korean meditation in the United States. Following my inner voice, I wanted to deepen my understanding of American people and culture. This led me on a journey across the country, traveling from east to west. Eventually, I settled in Sedona, Arizona, where I took over an abandoned retreat center surrounded by stunning red rocks. This decision was inspired by a moment of insight while meditating on Bell Rock. Today, that retreat center is cherished by many as a place of healing and spiritual growth.

Over time, listening to my inner voice has become second nature. Each time I follow it, I meet new people, discover new opportunities, and open a new chapter in my life. When we turn on our BrainPhones and take action guided by our inner voice, we unlock the incredible potential of our brains to transform our lives and create meaningful change.

Beyond Knowledge, Toward Fulfillment

What makes the BrainPhone special is that it connects us to information different from the knowledge we gather from typical outside sources. While most of what we know comes from experiences, books, the internet, or lectures, the wisdom we access through the BrainPhone is already within us. When we activate it, we're not creating something new but uncovering answers that have always been there. It's not about learning more; it's about reconnecting with our brain and rediscovering our inner wisdom.

Historically, we've used our brains mainly to gather and analyze knowledge, but with the rise of AI, that role is becoming less important. In some ways, AI has already surpassed humans in its ability to collect, process, and organize information.

Experts believe that general-purpose artificial intelligence (AGI) could soon become a reality. AGI refers to highly adaptable AI that can outperform humans in many areas, not just specific tasks. For example, AlphaGo, the AI that defeated Lee Sedol in Go, is brilliant at that one game but can't do anything else. AGI, however, could work across different fields and handle complex tasks, much like humans.

Some experts warn that AGI could grow uncontrollably through exponential learning, potentially outperforming human intelligence and spiraling out of control. This possibility has led Geoffrey Hinton, often called the "Godfather of AI," to warn that AI could be more dangerous than nuclear weapons.

In a time when AI is exceeding humans in almost every field, we must ask these questions: What makes the human brain valuable? Where does our true value come from?

The ultimate value of being human isn't measured by how much knowledge we accumulate—it's rooted in our mind and the wisdom it reveals. Knowledge, on its own, can't give us purpose or direction. In a world flooded with information, it's not the facts or data but the inner wisdom that helps us discern what truly matters and how to move forward. Wisdom goes beyond simply possessing information; it's the ability to understand and apply it meaningfully to our lives. Without wisdom, knowledge remains disconnected and unable to guide us toward a fulfilling and purposeful life.

The BrainPhone transforms the brain from a storehouse of knowledge into a gateway to our most profound wisdom and spiritual essence. By activating it, we unlock the brain's full potential, unleashing boundless creativity and energy. While AI handles tasks and processes knowledge, it cannot replicate what makes us human—our spiritual depth and inner wisdom. Our worth lies not in information or material success but in accessing and embodying the power of our minds. The BrainPhone guides us back to this inner strength and reclaims our limitless potential.

Unlike smartphones, which require constant updates to improve, the BrainPhone comes fully complete. It's a natural gift we are born with. It can generate creative solutions and wisdom from within without relying on anything external. In this way, it's fundamentally different from artificial systems. No matter how advanced or sophisticated a man-made system is, it's never truly complete. But life, by its nature, is complete and whole.

Just as a tree grows and a flower blooms on its own, we each possess an innate completeness, free spirit, and boundless creativity. Activating the BrainPhone unleashes this natural power, helping us shape the life and world we desire. The BrainPhone is fully formed within us and ready to be used. All we need to do is recognize its potential, turn it on, and let its light shine.

CHAPTER 3

LIFE IS A GAME OF BRAIN SPORTS

Our daily lives are often filled with routines that can feel mundane or uninspiring. But what if those quiet, ordinary moments held the key to reclaiming our minds? What if simple, intentional actions could reconnect us to ourselves, align us with our goals, and awaken untapped potential?

As we learned in the previous chapter, activating the BrainPhone transforms these seemingly ordinary moments into powerful chances to expand our potential. The BrainPhone is a natural system that connects us to our inner wisdom and potential, guiding us toward a more intentional way of living.

Everything we do is shaped by the brain—it's the center of our thoughts, actions, and experiences. This understanding inspired my work in developing Brain Education, a mind-body training system designed to help people harness their brain's full potential. While it has evolved into an academic discipline studied at the doctoral level, my primary goal has always been to make it practical and accessible for everyday life.

Building on this foundation, I propose Brain Sports: a practice of brain-centered life skills that activate the BrainPhone and promote a lifestyle of intentional living. Brain Sports fully engages the brain, turning everyday tasks into opportunities for growth and self-discovery. By combining intention and focus, it transforms daily actions into tools for improving well-being, inspiring creativity, and building emotional resilience. With Brain Sports, routine moments become meaningful exercises that unlock potential and lead to a more balanced, fulfilling life.

Brain Sports integrates the brain into every aspect of life, emphasizing its central role in all we do. The word "brain" highlights this connection, while "sports" inspires a positive, growth-oriented mindset. Like traditional sports that build strength and resilience through consistent effort, Brain Sports helps us develop practical skills, navigate challenges, and support our overall well-being.

Unlike traditional sports, which focus on physical competition, Brain Sports embraces a broader spectrum of activities. These range from physical exercises, such as strength training or stretching, to mental practices like meditation or problem-solving, as well as creative pursuits like painting or playing music. Brain Sports brings the BrainPhone into daily life, creating a framework for intentional living through focus, creativity, and mindfulness.

Brain Sports reframes daily routines into engaging challenges, encouraging personal growth and creativity. The key is setting your own goals and rules and turning simple tasks into meaningful avenues for self-development. By intentionally activating your

BrainPhone during these activities, you can amplify focus and clarity, and deepen your connection with yourself.

Through Brain Sports, the BrainPhone becomes a guide for intentional living by helping you engage fully in everyday activities. For example, reorganizing your workspace can go beyond just tidying up—it's an opportunity to think creatively about how to make your environment more functional and inspiring. A simple walk can become a mindful practice by focusing on your breath, noticing how your steps create a natural rhythm, or paying attention to the sounds and sensations around you. Even cooking a meal can be a fun challenge, whether you're experimenting with new flavors or creatively using what's in your pantry.

By adding intention, mindfulness, and personalized goals to everyday actions, Brain Sports transforms simple moments into powerful pathways for growth, self-discovery, and unlocking your BrainPhone's limitless potential.

Restoring the Spirit of Sports

Throughout history, sports have been more than games—they have shaped societies, built character, and strengthened communities. In both Eastern and Western civilizations, sports were physical activities and practices that harmonized the body and mind, fostered virtues, and held cultural or even sacred significance.

In ancient Greece, the Olympics exemplified these values. Besides being physical contests, the games were celebrations of unity and peace. Wars were paused, and city-states united to honor ideals like respect, humility, and courage. The Greeks viewed sports as a balance of physical strength, intellectual sharpness, and moral character that inspired personal excellence while nurturing collective harmony.

In the East, sports emphasized balance and community, drawing from principles like Tao and humaneness. Activities focused on living in harmony with nature and cultivating virtues such as empathy, responsibility, and compassion. These practices nurtured individuals while fostering shared growth and purpose within communities.

Today, more people than ever participate in sports and fitness, yet the deeper purpose of sports has often been overshadowed. The global sports industry focuses heavily on competition, commercialism, and celebrity culture. Professional leagues and star athletes dominate the spotlight, turning sports into entertainment spectacles. While this inspires many to stay active, it shifts the focus away from the core values of sports—bringing people together, building character, and creating a sense of community.

Brain Sports seeks to bring back the deeper purpose of sports as a way to connect, grow, and find balance in our daily lives. It reimagines harmony, character-building, and community values, not as distant ideals but as practices we can embrace in simple, everyday actions. Unlike the highly competitive nature of modern sports, Brain Sports focuses on participation and progress, inviting everyone—regardless of age or ability—to take part. Whether finding joy in mindful movement, strengthening bonds through shared activities, or fostering resilience through small challenges, Brain Sports offers a way to rediscover the essence of what sports were meant to be: a celebration of effort, connection, and the potential within each of us.

From Reaction to Creation

Brain Sports is rooted in the understanding that while the brain processes all our experiences, the mind gives them meaning and direction. From simple actions like walking or eating to reflecting on challenges or imagining a better future, the brain provides the stage, but the mind decides what to focus on and how to respond, shaping the stories of our lives.

In the rush of daily life, the mind's role often takes a backseat as the brain operates on autopilot. Automatic reactions—snapping in frustration, endlessly scrolling through social media to avoid discomfort, or overeating to suppress emotions—are common examples of the brain running without the mind's conscious guidance. Over time, this reactive way of living can disconnect us from our true desires and prevent us from making meaningful, intentional choices.

Brain Sports help break this cycle by training the mind to work actively with the brain. It doesn't require grand changes—small, intentional steps can have a powerful impact. For example, reframing a stressful situation as a challenge to grow, practicing gratitude to shift your emotional state, or engaging in mindful stretching to release tension are ways to integrate Brain Sports into daily life. These activities strengthen the mind's ability to guide the brain, allowing us to move from passive reactions to active creation.

We can navigate life's challenges with greater clarity and resilience by fostering a stronger connection between the mind and brain. This practice helps us move beyond reactive habits, embrace intentional living, and create a life that meaningfully reflects our values and aspirations.

Turning Life into Brain Sports

Sports are more than physical activities—they are about embracing challenges, discovering potential, and growing stronger through effort. Similarly, every part of life can become a sport. Whether managing relationships, solving problems, or learning new skills, life consistently presents opportunities to engage your brain, body, and mind. These opportunities aren't limited to physical activity; they extend into mental, social, and spiritual areas, offering countless chances to learn and grow.

Even ordinary actions like drinking water or getting dressed hold growth potential when approached with awareness and intention. With Brain Sports, life's challenges become arenas to test your limits and expand your capabilities. Every moment, whether routine or extraordinary, carries the essence of a sport, giving you the chance to awaken your inner potential.

Physical activity remains a powerful way to engage in Brain Sports. Movements like running, swimming, or hiking challenge your endurance and build strength, while even lighter actions, such as walking or stretching, energize your body and sharpen your focus. These activities enhance physical health, boost mood, and awaken mental clarity.

Mental activities are equally significant. Tackling a complex problem, reading something thought-provoking, or brainstorming new ideas trains your brain to adapt and grow. These moments enhance creativity, improve concentration, and help you build resilience.

Social interactions add another dimension to Brain Sports. Engaging in meaningful conversations, offering empathy, deep listening, or collaborating with others strengthens relationships while building emotional intelligence and cognitive flexibility. These everyday experiences remind us of the power of connection in shaping both the mind and heart.

Spiritual activities, like meditation, prayer, or quiet reflection, provide opportunities to connect with yourself and find your greater purpose. These practices nurture self-awareness, inner peace, and clarity, helping you align your actions with your values and intentions.

Brain Sports help us view life as an ongoing journey of growth. Approaching each day with curiosity and purpose—through movement, thought, connection, or reflection—turns daily challenges into meaningful steps toward greater intention and balance.

Aligning Mind and Body

In today's fast-paced world, life often feels fragmented. We separate work, family, and personal goals, losing sight of how they influence and support one another. Even within ourselves, we divide the mind and body—sometimes focusing on mental tasks while neglecting physical activities that ground and energize us. This fragmented approach leaves us feeling unbalanced, stretched thin, and disconnected from a sense of fulfillment.

Brain Sports challenge this separation by emphasizing integration. It is rooted in the understanding that all physical, mental, and spiritual activities are interconnected through the brain and body. When approached with intention, these activities create opportunities to align our thoughts, emotions, and actions, promoting harmony and growth. This integrative perspective turns every moment into a chance to cultivate balance, self-discovery, and resilience.

The disconnect between mind and body is often visible in how we approach physical activity. For example, running on a treadmill while watching TV or scrolling through a phone keeps the body active but leaves the mind disengaged. This common habit limits the potential benefits of movement by missing the opportunity to deepen the connection between mind and body. Bridging this gap begins with mindful engagement—aligning physical actions with mental focus and awareness.

Next time you go for a run, whether on a treadmill or in a park, pay close attention to your body. Notice the sensations in your muscles, the movement of your joints, and the rhythm of your breath. Feel the tension and relaxation as your body moves. This focused awareness strengthens the connection between your brain and body. You can take it further by imagining energy flowing through you with each step, reinforcing your strength and focus. Studies show that engaging your brain during physical activity enhances physical performance, sharpens focus, and improves mental resilience.

Like running, any everyday movement can become a powerful opportunity for integration when done mindfully. Performing a squat with awareness improves movement quality, walking with focus enhances creativity, and mindful stretching promotes relaxation and body awareness. Even small actions like climbing stairs with more awareness improve coordination and build neural connections.

The core of Brain Sports lies in this integrative mindset. It recognizes that every activity is part of a unified experience. By approaching life with the understanding that nothing is separate, we can connect our physical health, mental clarity, and spiritual fulfillment into a balanced whole.

Embracing Purposeful Resistance

In nature, water and electricity follow the path of least resistance, effortlessly choosing the easiest way forward. Humans often do the same, opting for comfort and convenience. While this saves energy, relying too much on the easy path can lead to stagnation, dulling our ability to adapt and robbing us of growth opportunities. Modern technology makes this even more tempting, automating challenges and reducing our engagement. While these tools make life easier, they can also limit our potential by encouraging passivity.

Actual growth requires purposeful resistance—intentionally choosing challenges that stretch and develop us. This doesn't mean making life harder unnecessarily; it's about embracing meaningful challenges that foster resilience, creativity, and self-discovery. Purposeful resistance builds character and unlocks potential, helping us grow stronger in every aspect of life.

Purposeful resistance can take many forms. Physically, it might involve starting a new fitness routine or training for a marathon. Mentally, it could mean learning a difficult skill or tackling a complex project. Emotionally, it might involve facing fears, having tough conversations, or practicing vulnerability.

While these challenges may feel uncomfortable at first, each one is an opportunity for growth, training you to adapt, persevere, and thrive.

Sports offer a clear metaphor for purposeful resistance. Athletes push their limits by lifting heavier weights, running faster, or perfecting their skills. These efforts build strength and resilience. Brain Sports applies this same principle to daily life, turning challenges into meaningful opportunities for personal growth. By embracing these challenges with curiosity and purpose, you strengthen your body, mind, and spirit, just as athletes strengthen their physical capabilities.

Like a salmon swimming upstream, growth often requires resisting the easy flow and embracing effort and persistence. The path of least resistance may feel safe, but it rarely leads to transformation. Purposeful resistance unlocks hidden strengths, builds character, and opens doors to new possibilities. By incorporating intentional challenges into your daily life, Brain Sports empowers you to grow stronger, more creative, and more resilient.

The Heart of Brain Sports

Brain Sports puts each of us at the center of the game, making us the star players in our own lives. This isn't about self-centeredness—it's about embracing personal growth and creating a meaningful life. By focusing on our own progress, we build momentum and motivation. Just as fans cheer for their favorite athletes, we can learn to support and celebrate our own efforts and achievements, recognizing that every step forward matters.

Brain Sports are for everyone, unlike traditional sports, which often prioritize the young, the elite, or the physically strong. Life itself becomes the ultimate playing field, where the goal is not to outperform others but to strive to improve ourselves each day. Whether it's a child learning a new skill, an adult building resilience, or a senior staying active, Brain Sports provide a framework for discovering potential and living with intention at every stage of life.

The heart of Brain Sports lies in small, consistent actions that bring meaning and satisfaction. Progress might look like doing one more pull-up, finishing a long-overdue project, or simply offering a kind word to someone in need. By activating the BrainPhone in these moments, we can align our intentions with our actions, deepening our focus and enhancing our connection to the task at hand. Brain Sports emphasizes working at your own pace, celebrating milestones, and finding joy in the journey rather than focusing on competition or external measures of success.

Brain Sports also cultivates a spirit of collective growth. In contrast to traditional sports, which often spotlight individual achievements, Brain Sports highlights the importance of mutual support and encouragement. Activating the BrainPhone allows us to access greater empathy and understanding, helping others succeed while strengthening our own growth. This creates a culture of collaboration and shared progress, enriching both our communities and our sense of connection to one another.

At its core, Brain Sports transforms life into an integrated and balanced adventure. By aligning the mind and body and approaching daily activities with curiosity and purpose, Brain

Sports helps us cultivate inner strength, ignite creativity, and deepen our connections with ourselves and others.

The BrainPhone amplifies this process, guiding us to greater clarity, balance, and fulfillment. This isn't about being the fastest, the strongest, or the best—it's about embracing life fully and becoming the best version of ourselves.

When we see life through the lens of Brain Sports, every moment becomes an opportunity to discover our potential, foster resilience, and live with greater intention. By playing the starring role in our lives, we unlock our true capabilities and inspire those around us to do the same. Brain Sports celebrates the power of growth, connection, and purpose, turning life into an arena of transformation and fulfillment.

CHAPTER 4

ALIGN YOUR INNER VIBRATION

To turn on your BrainPhone and unlock its full potential, it's essential to understand that it works through the natural principles of vibration and resonance. Like tuning a radio to a clear frequency or harmonizing an instrument, your BrainPhone picks up on the subtle vibrations within you and shapes your thoughts, emotions, and energy.

These vibrations influence how you feel and interact with the world around you. By engaging in Brain Sports, you activate your BrainPhone and learn to notice and adjust these vibrations. This practice helps you create a sense of balance and clarity, allowing you to feel more connected to yourself and your surroundings.

Everything Is a Vibration

Everything in the world is fundamentally a vibration. From the smallest particles of matter to the vast expanse of the universe, everything consists of energy that moves and vibrates. Even our thoughts, feelings, and sensations are essentially patterns of energy in motion. All living beings, along with seemingly inanimate objects like books or chairs, are made up of tiny particles that vibrate constantly. These vibrations are what gives matter its structure and form. If this movement were to stop, matter would cease to exist as we know it, and the physical reality we experience would dissolve.

Observation of sound and vibration offers a simple demonstration of this concept. If you sprinkle fine sand or salt on a plate and expose it to specific sound frequencies, the vibrations cause the grains to arrange themselves into intricate patterns. As the frequency increases, the patterns become more complex. This shows that vibration isn't just about movement—it has the power to create and shape forms.

On a much larger scale, the universe itself began with a vibration—the Big Bang. This massive explosion of energy gave rise to time, space, matter, and life. In many ways, the vibrations from that moment continue to resonate through everything we see and experience today.

Ancient wisdom across cultures has recognized the foundational role of vibration. In the *Budoji*, an ancient Korean text, heaven and earth arise from a primordial vibration called *yullyeo*. Similarly, the Bible describes creation beginning with God speaking a word, suggesting the power of sound as a creative force. In Eastern philosophy, the natural flow and transformation of the universe is called Tao, which works through the interaction of two opposing yet complementary forces, yin and yang. This interaction can also be understood as a form of vibration.

Vibration is at the heart of life and existence. From the orbit of planets to the cycles of the seasons, the tides, the phases of the moon, the blooming of flowers, and even the rhythm of our breathing—all are expressions of vibration. On every level, from the microscopic to the cosmic, vibration connects and organizes the universe, shaping our world.

Everything Has a Unique Vibration

Everything in the world has its own vibration. Differences in size, shape, and material give every object a unique frequency. Just like fingerprints are unique to each person, objects like desks, cups, and even the smallest grains of sand have their own distinct and specific vibrations.

In the human body, every cell has its own vibration. When these vibrations are stable and balanced, the cells function properly. However, stress or illness can disrupt these vibrations, leading to instability. For example, when we're stressed, our heart might race, our breathing might become shallow, or we might feel tired or in pain. These are signs that our body has shifted out of its natural state of balance.

Organs also rely on specific rhythms and vibrations to function. Our heart beats steadily to pump blood, our brain sends signals as electrical waves, our lungs expand and contract to bring in oxygen and remove carbon dioxide, and our intestines move food along with regular contractions. If these vibrations are altered, it can affect our health.

Vibrations are essential for keeping the body and mind healthy. They help things work properly and show us when something is wrong. Some types of medicine, like wave therapy, use light or sound to rebalance the body's vibrations and support healing. Even traditional treatments like acupuncture work by helping the body restore its natural energy flow and rhythm.

Vibrations of Emotions

Our emotions, just like our cells and organs, are expressed as energy and vibration. Each emotion has its unique vibration, which directly affects our overall energy.

Positive emotions like joy, love, and gratitude tend to have a high vibration. When we feel these emotions, our body and mind become energized, and our energy flows more smoothly. These emotions also trigger the release of hormones like endorphins, serotonin, and oxytocin. These feel-good hormones lift our mood and help our cells repair and regenerate.

For instance, when we feel love, we often experience a sense of warmth and comfort that generates positive energy throughout the body. This energy helps our cells, including immune cells, function more effectively, strengthening our immune system and making it better at protecting us from illness and stress. Positive emotions also improve blood circulation, stabilize heart rate, and regulate breathing, which supports overall physical health. This is why feelings of love and joy often leave us feeling lighter, healthier, and more at ease.

Negative emotions like fear, anger, and sadness tend to have a lower vibration, which blocks energy flow and can negatively affect the body. These negative emotions often make us feel heavy and tired. When they last long, stress hormones such as cortisol are released, weakening the immune system and making us more vulnerable to illness.

Emotions like sadness or fear can also cause muscle tension and irregular breathing. This stress then disrupts the flow of energy, making the heart rate unstable, raising blood pressure, and causing digestive issues. It can also affect sleep, leading to insomnia. If these emotions persist, they can contribute to mental health issues like depression and anxiety.

All the elements that make up our body and mind have their own unique vibration, and together, they create our overall vibration. We often use words like *vibe*, *feeling*, or *energy* to describe the impression we get from a person or place. For example, when we say, "He had such good energy," or "I had a really good feeling around them," or "I can feel her vibe," we're picking up on the unique vibrations that person is giving off.

Our vibration is not fixed; it constantly changes based on our thoughts, emotions, and state of mind and body. When we're in a good or bad mood, tense or relaxed, our vibration shifts accordingly. Our brain and body always send out energy, which influences our surroundings and the people we interact with.

The BrainPhone works based on these vibrations. Like a smartphone senses our movement and location, the BrainPhone picks up on our vibrations, helping us become aware of our energy state. Vibrations aren't just random bursts of energy; they are a language the brain uses to connect our inner feelings with the outside world. Using the BrainPhone is about learning to understand and use this language to take back your brain.

Every living and nonliving thing has a unique vibration, but what makes humans different is our ability to recognize and adjust our vibration consciously. We can feel our thoughts, emotions, and physical states through vibrations, and we have the power to change them through our choices and actions.

For example, we know when our energy feels heavy and unstable due to stress or anxiety. Instead of staying in that state, we can take deep breaths or go for a walk to shift our energy from a heavy, unstable vibration to a lighter, more balanced one.

Recognizing and adjusting our own vibration means we can shape our lives. By being mindful of our thoughts, emotions, and energy, we take back the power to choose and change the direction of our lives. When we use our BrainPhones to tap into this power, we stop just reacting to our environments and start transforming our experiences.

The Power of Resonance

In addition to vibration, another key principle of the BrainPhone is resonance. Resonance happens when two or more vibrations meet and affect each other, causing them to either strengthen or weaken. This effect is powerful and can be seen in the physical world and in our emotions and relationships.

You've probably seen the tuning fork experiment in school: tapping one tuning fork creates a vibration at a particular frequency. If there's another tuning fork nearby with the same frequency, it will start vibrating on its own—without being tapped. This phenomenon happens because the two tuning forks are in resonance, and their vibrations grow stronger when their frequencies match.

A well-known example of resonance's power is the 1940 collapse of the Narrows Bridge in Tacoma, Washington. The bridge suddenly gave way just months after it opened because the wind, blowing at 40 miles per hour, matched the bridge's natural frequency. The vibrations grew stronger until the structure couldn't handle them anymore, and it began to sway uncontrollably, eventually collapsing.

A similar incident happened in 1831 with the Broughton Suspension Bridge in England. At the time, 74 soldiers marched across the bridge in step, and their footsteps matched the bridge's natural frequency. This created resonance, causing the bridge to sway violently and eventually collapse. While no one died, many soldiers fell into the water and were injured. As a result, the British military introduced a rule for soldiers to break step when crossing bridges.

When vibrations are in sync, they resonate, increasing their energy. This effect happens not only within ourselves but also in our relationships and in the spaces around us. Like how a tuning fork amplifies sound, our vibrations interact with the people and environment around us, either amplifying or dampening them. Collective emotions, like the mood of a group, can become stronger through this resonance. For example, when one person bursts into laughter, it's contagious, creating a domino effect that lifts everyone's spirits. The positive vibration of laughter resonates and boosts the energy of the group.

On the other hand, negative emotions can spread just as quickly through resonance. When someone expresses anger or anxiety, others nearby may feel the same energy. Thus, negative emotions tend to grow stronger in conflict situations, fueled by fear or anxiety. On social media or in online communities, a post filled with anger or frustration can quickly lead to a chain reaction, with others sharing similar feelings, escalating the conflict and division further.

One of the most powerful examples of emotional resonance happens at a sporting event or concert. For instance, when a player takes a shot at the goal during a tense soccer game, everyone holds their breath, watching the ball closely. The moment the ball hits the net, a wave of energy rushes through the crowd like an electric jolt.

Immediately, cheers and shouts erupt, and people jump to their feet, high-fiving, hugging, and celebrating together. They read each other's excitement, and those emotions build on each other, creating a powerful vibration of energy. The entire stadium seems to resonate with this energy as if everyone is breathing in sync, sharing the same rhythm. This shared vibration feeds into the players, creating a strong connection between the crowd and the game. At that moment, everyone in the stadium is in resonance, experiencing the same powerful emotions.

When we understand that our vibrations have a powerful impact on others, we become more mindful of managing our own energy and its effect on the collective energy around us.

When we resonate with positive vibrations, we create healthier relationships, uplift each other, and share more energy and vitality. This positive flow of emotions and energy creates a cycle that helps us grow personally and encourages positive change in the wider community.

On the other hand, resonating with negative vibrations can lead to discomfort, conflict, and chaos. By being mindful of the effect of our vibrations and focusing on spreading positive energy, we can improve not only our own lives but also the lives of those we interact with.

Harmonizing Your Vibrations

Natural vibrations within our bodies—like heartbeats, brain waves, and subtle shifts in energy—are honest reflections of our inner state. These vibrations constantly change based on how we feel and respond to the world around us. Unlike temporary signals like facial expressions or gestures that can be faked, these internal vibrations are more subtle and truthful, showing us the connection between our inner experiences and the energy we project outward.

The BrainPhone operates by sensing these vibrations and helping us become aware of them. For instance, when we're calm, our heart beats steadily, and our brain waves slow into a relaxed rhythm. In contrast, stress or anxiety might quicken our pulse, tense our muscles, or disrupt our breathing. These vibrations don't just reflect how we feel; they also shape how we interact with others and influence the choices we make.

Our thoughts, emotions, and physical sensations create unique vibrations that align with certain possibilities in life. For example, when you feel anxious, it might attract more tension and challenges. On the other hand, cultivating gratitude or optimism can create a sense of calm and open new opportunities. This alignment isn't coincidental—it's the result of how our internal energy resonates with the environment around us. By recognizing and adjusting these vibrations, we gain the ability to shape our experiences more intentionally.

This is where Brain Sports play a vital role. Brain Sports are practical tools that help turn on your BrainPhone, calibrate it, and amplify its signal so it can better sense, regulate, and refine your vibrations. Through activities that encourage balance and focus—like gentle movement, deep breathing, or moments of quiet observation—your BrainPhone can better calm scattered energy and restore harmony. These practices act like tuning tools for your BrainPhone, helping it align your inner state with your intentions.

When paired with Brain Sports, the BrainPhone becomes more effective. Just as a well-tuned instrument sustains clear and harmonious sound, regular practice helps your inner vibrations resonate more positively. Brain Sports don't just help in moments of stress or distraction; they also create a foundation for mental clarity and emotional stability through consistent effort.

Engaging with your BrainPhone through Brain Sports is simple and powerful. Small adjustments, like taking a deep breath to reset your energy or replacing a negative thought with a constructive one, can make a noticeable difference in how you feel and respond. These moments of tuning in and recalibrating create lasting benefits, helping you approach life with greater intention and balance.

Take a moment now to check in with yourself using your BrainPhone. How does your energy feel—calm or restless, light or heavy? If something feels off, think about how you might adjust it. A deep breath, a brisk walk, or simply pausing to observe your thoughts can help realign your vibration. These small, intentional actions may seem simple, but over time, they build a strong foundation for a more centered and fulfilling life.

By consciously managing your vibrations through the BrainPhone and Brain Sports, you can align your inner world with the life you want to create. This alignment not only helps you navigate challenges with greater ease but also empowers you to bring clarity, resilience, and purpose to your everyday experiences.

Connecting to Inner Feelings

The vibrations that the BrainPhone detects go beyond surface-level thoughts, emotions, or physical sensations. They tap into something more profound, which I'll call "inner feelings." These deeper vibrations reflect who we are, what we truly want, and the direction we should take in life. They form the foundation of our inner and spiritual awareness.

Feelings, in general, are the emotions or sensations we experience daily—like happiness, sadness, anger, or physical sensations such as warmth or cold. These feelings usually arise in response to specific situations or our environment and tend to be temporary and ever-changing.

Inner feelings, on the other hand, are deeper and more steady. They come from within and aren't just reactions to what's happening around us. These feelings are more intuitive and often guide us in ways that don't always make logical sense. Yet, we usually trust them because they feel authentic and align with something deeper inside us.

How we feel inside plays a crucial role in understanding our thoughts, choices, and actions. Our inner feelings are the final verdict on whether something is right for us—they determine whether a decision truly aligns with our authentic desires. The accurate measure of whether something is right for us is how it makes us feel on the inside.

For example, imagine achieving a goal you've worked hard for—whether it's a new home, a promotion, or a relationship you've longed for. But how do you know if this accomplishment is truly what you wanted? While praise or recognition from others can be satisfying and may make you feel like you made the right choice, your inner feelings ultimately tell you if the achievement is truly meaningful to you.

If you still feel empty after reaching your goal or sense that something is missing, it's likely a sign that it doesn't align with your true desires. You might push those feelings aside at first, but if they continue to grow, you'll eventually have to face the fact that what you thought you wanted may not truly fulfill you.

Of course, realizing that what you feel inside is true doesn't mean everyone acts on it. Some people ask themselves, "What do I really want?" and let go of what they have, dream new dreams, and work toward making them happen. But many others ignore that feeling and stay where they are, sticking with what's familiar.

However, we can't ignore our inner truths forever. There will come a time when we look back, and the truths we've avoided will catch up with us. What seemed like satisfaction or hope at the moment can turn into regret or emptiness later, weighing heavily on us. In the end, we all must confront the truth of our lives. When, at the end of our lives, we face the question, "Did I live my life well?" what will our answer be?

The answer can never be the house we own, the car we drive, or the money in the bank because they don't stay with us forever. What often remains with us, however, are the feelings and experiences that shape our lives.

The goals we pursue or achievements we chase aren't the ultimate purpose—they are often driven by the way we want to feel. It might seem like we're seeking money or success, but beneath that, we may be longing for a sense of security, freedom, or pride. The same applies to relationships: people and experiences matter to us because of the love, connection, and joy they bring. That's why it's essential to reflect on the goals we set and understand the deeper feelings we're truly striving for.

Beyond Thoughts, Emotions, and Sensations

Inner feelings aren't thoughts, emotions, or physical sensations. When our minds are overwhelmed with busy thoughts, strong emotions, or intense sensory experiences, it can be difficult to notice our inner feelings.

Our thoughts tend to focus on analyzing, judging, and labeling things as right or wrong. In doing so, we unwittingly create more stress and anxiety for ourselves by overthinking and worrying about the outcome. For example, before an important meeting, thoughts like, "Are my materials good enough?" or "How will my coworkers see me?" can add unnecessary pressure, even before the meeting starts.

Emotions are strong forces that can easily override our rational thinking. We've all experienced moments when we've said something hurtful in the heat of an argument, only to regret it later. Emotions push us to react quickly; when we let them take control, we miss the opportunity to pause and make better choices.

Similarly, intense physical sensations, whether pain or pleasure, can distract our attention from what's important. If we suddenly feel pain or discomfort, we focus so much on that sensation that we forget what's happening around us or what we were doing. These distractions can make it harder to make clear, balanced decisions.

Inner feelings work differently from thoughts, emotions, and physical sensations. They don't analyze or judge like thoughts, demand immediate reactions like emotions, or narrow our focus like physical sensations. Instead, they guide our awareness inward. When focusing on our inner feelings, we don't fixate on a particular thought, emotion, or sensation. We're tuning in to a more profound sense of ourselves while staying connected to everything around us.

Trying to notice our inner feelings while our mind is full of thoughts, emotions are running high, or we're distracted by intense physical sensations is like trying to hear a leaf rustling in the wind when surrounded by loud city noises. The sound is there, but the distractions make it hard to pick up. When our thoughts are quiet, our emotions are balanced, and we're not overwhelmed by external stimuli, we can hear our inner feelings more clearly.

The Source of Inner Feelings

If you've ever practiced meditation or self-reflection regularly, you've probably experienced a moment when your thoughts slow down, your emotions settle, and you're not as affected by outside distractions. In that moment, your focus shifts from what's happening around you to what's happening inside you.

This shift can be reflected in brain activity—moving from the usual, busy beta waves to more relaxed alpha waves and deeper into meditation's theta and delta waves. In this relaxed state, your thoughts, emotions, and sensations slow down, and your inner feelings become clearer. It's like stepping away from a noisy street into a peaceful forest, where you can finally hear the leaves rustling in the wind.

These inner feelings might present as a sense of peace, relief, clarity, or firm conviction. But not all inner feelings are positive at first. Sometimes, when we calm down, we may encounter emotions or unresolved issues we've been avoiding. These feelings may seem confusing or uncomfortable initially, but they are just as important. Discomfort often points us toward truths we need to face. Over time, these challenging feelings can lead to clarity, offering opportunities for growth and healing. What feels unclear or complicated at first can eventually guide us toward a more profound understanding and personal transformation.

Sometimes, our inner feelings lead us to ask ourselves important questions. We sense something inside and wonder, "Are my choices right for me?" or "Is this what I really want?" Whether the feelings are positive or challenging, they help us check in with ourselves, ensuring we're staying true to what really matters and guiding us toward more authentic choices.

Where do these inner feelings come from, and how can we trust them? At a fundamental level, we are all connected to a deeper wisdom and energy that shapes the universe. What we experience as inner feeling is actually a reflection of this energy flowing through us. Whether we're aware of it or not, this energy is always moving within us. When our mind is calm and free from distractions, we can feel this deeper energy more clearly, just like how the surface of a lake clears up when the ripples settle. This inner feeling is the universe's way of giving us feedback—it's the voice of our soul guiding us.

We are trying to sense and connect with these inner feelings through the BrainPhone. By paying attention to these feelings and learning to trust them, we align ourselves with the energy of the universe.

The GPS in Your Brain

This connection to our inner vibration—the voice of our soul—guides us in navigating life and making choices that resonate with our true desires. Our inner feelings act like a GPS, offering guidance from the deeper, wiser part of us connected to universal energy. When we face a challenging situation, and our inner feelings confirm, "This is the way to go," they become a powerful force, helping us confidently move toward our goals.

Through our BrainPhone, we can tune in to these subtle yet clear signals our brain transmits. Recognizing and following these signals is a shortcut to taking back control of our brain and making confident decisions. They will guide us with a clear, often powerful certainty beyond the understanding of the rational mind if we trust them.

By incorporating Brain Sports into your routine, you create an environment where your BrainPhone can work at its best, allowing your inner feelings to guide you more effortlessly. These practices strengthen the connection between your body and mind, creating the clarity and balance needed to hear and trust your inner GPS. Once you've aligned your vibrations and attuned to your inner feelings, you are ready to take the next step: transforming these aligned feelings into powerful, actionable visions through imagination. This is where the BrainPhone truly shines—not only as a tool for clarity but also as a gateway to creating the life you envision.

CHAPTER 5

ENERGIZE YOUR IMAGINATION

By turning on your BrainPhone and tuning in to your inner feelings, you gain clarity and confidence in making decisions that align with your true desires. But the power of inner feelings doesn't stop there—they unlock your imagination, one of the brain's most remarkable tools for creating change.

When you align yourself with your inner feelings, imagination transforms into a tool for creation. It bridges the gap between where you are and where you want to be, enabling you to envision what doesn't yet exist as if it already does.

This process begins with a single, powerful question: "What if…?" Steve Jobs asked this when imagining a device that could do everything in the palm of your hand. Martin Luther King envisioned a world where equality became a lived reality. In each case, imagination was fueled by a deep connection to inner feelings—a desire to create meaningful change.

Imagination isn't just abstract thinking; it has measurable effects on the mind and body. For example, imagining your favorite meal can make your mouth water, while anticipating a high-pressure situation like a job interview can trigger a racing heart or sweaty palms. This mind-body connection illustrates imagination's power to shape reality.

Scientific studies further highlight how imagination can influence physical abilities. A 2014 study from Ohio University found that participants who visualized flexing their arms daily for four weeks increased their strength significantly—without lifting a single weight. Similarly, the placebo effect demonstrates how belief and imagination can activate the body's natural healing processes.

Athletes have long harnessed this power through visualization training. Muhammad Ali imagined himself victorious in the ring, building his confidence and focus. Michael Phelps, the most decorated Olympian, visualized every detail of his races, from the feel of the water to handling unexpected challenges like a goggle malfunction. This mental practice prepared him to perform at his peak under pressure.

While imagination is a powerful starting point, it doesn't work alone. Turning aspirations into reality requires effort, planning, and concrete action. Yet imagination provides the foundation—it ignites the spark that transforms vague desires into clear, focused visions. When aligned with your inner feelings and strengthened through Brain Sports, imagination becomes even more impactful. These practices channel your energy and focus, shifting you from merely wishing for a better life to actively creating it. This chapter explores how to harness and amplify your imagination by combining it with the clarity of inner feelings and the discipline of Brain Sports.

The Power of Wanting

Desiring something is the starting point for growth and progress. Desire is a natural force that drives us to change our habits and work toward our goals. Without it, life becomes routine and stagnant, and we lack the energy to move forward.

Wanting is the foundation of motivation. Every action we take starts with a desire for something. For example, if you want to be healthier, you might change your diet or start exercising because you have a strong reason to improve your health. Without that desire, you will likely stay in your comfort zone and avoid making changes. Wanting is the spark that ignites all transformation. Even the slightest change won't happen unless you want it.

Behind every act of imagination and creation lies the force of wanting. A deep desire inspires us to picture what we want and moves us to act. When we want something strongly, we don't just dream about it; we work to make it real. Throughout history, people with strong desires have turned their aspirations into action. For instance, Mahatma Gandhi's profound wish for India's independence led him to organize a non-violent resistance movement. His determination inspired millions to join him, and their collective efforts eventually achieved independence for India.

To tap in to the power of imagination, you first need to understand what you want. While it might seem simple on the surface, truly knowing what you want can be challenging. We all have ordinary desires—things we want to own, eat, or accomplish. But when asked, "What do you *really* want?" many people struggle to answer. Often, our wishes are vague, fleeting, or influenced by outside pressures rather than clear personal aspirations.

In reality, many people go through life unsure of what they really want, or they avoid acknowledging it. Sometimes, people chase goals shaped by others' expectations or societal norms rather than their own desires. Other times, they fear admitting what they want because it requires change, which often means leaving the safety of the familiar.

If you truly want to unlock the power of imagination, the first step is to get honest with yourself about what you want. When you're clear about your true desires, they become more than wishes—they turn into goals with purpose. A clear goal gives your imagination direction and focus, allowing you to visualize specific outcomes and map out the steps needed to achieve them. The stronger your desire, the greater your determination to pursue it, and the clearer your path to achieving it becomes. With a clear goal, your imagination becomes a powerful tool to explore possibilities, identify solutions, and stay motivated as you bring your vision to life.

So, how do you figure out what you really want? The answer isn't found outside of yourself. Only you can truly know what you want—it's not something anyone else can decide for you. To discover it, you need to look inward. As mentioned in the previous chapter, your inner feelings and vibrations hold the key to understanding what you genuinely desire. By paying attention to these subtle cues, you can gain clarity about what truly matters to you and align your actions with your deepest aspirations.

The Power of Feelings

What do you want in your life? Take a moment to make a quick list of things that have been on your mind. Don't overthink it—just write down whatever comes to you.

Some people might find it easy to answer this because they already know what they want and are working toward it. Others may still be figuring things out or feel unsure about their goals. That's okay. Big or small, we all have things we hope for, so take a few minutes to get comfortable and write down what you want.

Now, ask yourself, "What kind of feelings do I want to experience more of in my life?" Maybe it's happiness, confidence, peace, joy, love, freedom, fulfillment, or something else. It doesn't have to be just one thing—write down all the feelings that matter to you. If you're unsure where to start, think about a time when you felt genuinely good. What feelings or needs were being met in that moment? Considering this can help you uncover the feelings that truly matter to you.

Next, return to the goals you wrote down and ask yourself if they would bring you your desired feelings. For some goals, the answer might be a strong "yes." For others, it could be "no" or "I'm not sure." If you're unsure or realize that a goal might not bring you the feelings you want, ask yourself, "What could give me that feeling?" The answer might come quickly or take some time and reflection. Either way, that's fine—it's natural for this process to require more than one attempt. Give yourself the freedom to revisit this question over the coming days as clarity unfolds.

You may also notice that your priorities or values have shifted. Goals that once felt meaningful might not feel the same anymore. This doesn't mean you're lost; it's part of growing and understanding what truly drives you.

To make this practice even more effective, try linking your goals to the feelings behind them. For example, if you want to travel more, is it because you crave adventure, a sense of freedom, or the opportunity to connect with new cultures? Or, if you're striving to lose weight, is it because you want to feel healthier, more confident, or because there's something specific you'd like to do once you reach your goal? Understanding the connection between your goals and feelings helps you refine what truly matters and guides you toward actions aligned with your inner needs.

I encourage you to reflect on your feelings because, as mentioned in the previous chapter, your inner feelings are the most reliable guide for understanding where you are in life and what you truly want. They act like a GPS, pointing you toward your goals and values.

While our brain might second-guess our thoughts, it accepts feelings as they are. When you experience a feeling, the brain processes it as an actual event and sends signals throughout your body to respond. These signals cause physical changes, such as hormonal shifts, rapid heartbeat, and increased blood flow, making feelings a powerful link between the brain and body.

For example, think about the feeling of fear. When you imagine or face a threatening situation, your brain interprets the fear as a real danger. It sends signals to your body that speed up your heartbeat, make your palms sweat, and tense your muscles. These physical reactions intensify fear, creating a feedback loop where the feeling triggers physical changes, and those changes reinforce the feeling. This cycle shows how feelings can turn mental reactions into real physical effects.

Feelings are a powerful motivator for action. While thoughts alone don't always lead to action, strong feelings often do. When you feel hungry, you don't need to rationalize why you should eat—you just feel it and take action to find food. In contrast, merely thinking it's time to eat might not prompt the same immediate response. The same applies to exercise. Knowing that exercise is good for your health doesn't necessarily make you work out. But if you feel heavy or out of shape, that feeling can motivate you to take action and start exercising.

In this way, feelings drive behavior far more directly than thoughts. They are the most potent force influencing how we act and what we strive for. By paying attention to your feelings, you can better understand your motivations and align your actions with what holds true value for you.

Not only can feelings help us understand what we truly want, but they also make our imagination far more effective in achieving our goals. Since the ultimate purpose of any goal is to experience a specific feeling, such as happiness, freedom, or accomplishment, combining imagination with those feelings can amplify its power.

The Science of Visualization

In 1979, Dr. Ellen Langer of Harvard University conducted a study known as the Counterclockwise Experiment. It involved eight elderly men in their 70s and 80s who participated in a five-day retreat where everything was designed to resemble life 20 years earlier. One group was asked to reminisce about their younger days, while the other was instructed to act and talk as though they were actually living 20 years ago.

By the end of the retreat, both groups showed improvements, but the group that fully embraced "acting younger" saw more significant changes. They had better posture, more flexible joints, reduced arthritis, and even longer fingers, likely due to reduced joint swelling. Their eyesight, hearing, and memory improved as well. By the last day, men who had seemed frail and dependent were playing a game of touch football on the lawn. In just five days, their mindset and behavior led to real, measurable changes in their physical health and vitality.

This study highlights how powerful feelings can be when paired with imagination. The group that fully embodied their younger selves—thinking, acting, and feeling as if they were 20 years younger—experienced the most remarkable transformation. Their bodies responded to their mindset, showing how aligning feelings with imagination can make a profound difference.

Visualization is a proven tool for improving performance, especially in sports. The idea that imagining an action can make you better at it might sound like magic, but science backs it up. A 2019 study in the *Journal of Science and Medicine in Sport* revealed just how powerful mental imagery can be. From volleyball spikes to basketball shots and golf swings, athletes who used visualization techniques saw significant improvements in their skills. In fact, 90 percent of the studies reviewed reported clear performance boosts, proving that a well-trained mind is just as crucial as a well-trained body.

However, other studies suggest that the effectiveness of visualization depends on experience. For athletes, it's particularly effective because their bodies already know what the movement feels like. Years of practice create a strong connection between mental imagery and physical sensations, allowing the brain to activate the same neural pathways used during real practice. For example, when seasoned athletes imagine shooting a basketball or swinging a golf club, their bodies respond as if they are performing the action, reinforcing muscle memory and improving performance.

For non-athletes, however, the impact of visualization is less pronounced. Without prior experience or developed muscle memory, they often visualize passively—like watching a screen rather than fully engaging their bodies. This lack of connection makes it harder for visualization to translate into tangible improvements, though it can still provide some benefits.

The key to making visualization truly effective is adding feeling—not just picturing the image in your mind but fully engaging your body and emotions in the process. When you involve your senses, the image becomes vivid and lifelike, as if it's actually happening. This connection between imagination and physical and emotional sensations gives the practice depth and energy, making it even more impactful for achieving your goals.

From Wanting to Being

One of the most effective ways to imagine what you want is to focus on feelings that resonate with you personally. When your imagination connects to something meaningful, it naturally sticks and feels more real.

For example, if your goal is to succeed at work, focusing only on specific achievements like getting a promotion or a raise might feel detached or uninspiring. Instead, try visualizing moments that would truly matter to you: your team valuing your leadership, your coworkers expressing pride in working with you, or celebrating a big success together. These kinds of images carry emotional weight.

The same goes for imagining your dream home. Thinking only about its size, location, or cost might feel abstract. But picturing yourself having warm family dinners, enjoying peaceful evenings, or seeing your kids play in the yard can feel more tangible. Connecting with these specific moments gives your imagination depth and meaning.

The key is to make the experience feel real—not just a thought in your head but an experience that evokes emotion in the present moment. When you connect with that feeling, your body and mind respond as if it's already happening. This changes how you approach your goal, giving you energy and focus that make it easier to take steps toward it.

When you imagine, don't just think about what you want; imagine yourself as the person who has already achieved it. What would that feel like? How would you carry yourself? When you embody those feelings, you naturally align your actions and decisions with that version of yourself.

This is similar to how confident leaders inspire trust—not because they're trying to, but because they already carry leadership qualities. Or how people with an uplifting, friendly presence naturally attract others. It's not about wishing; it's about becoming.

Shifting your focus from wanting to being not only changes how you feel but also influences how you act. When you vividly imagine yourself living the life you want, whether it's a life of financial stability or creative fulfillment, you start aligning with that reality in your everyday choices.

For example, instead of simply wishing for more money, you might imagine the security and freedom it brings and start making decisions with that mindset. Or, instead of hoping to be more creative, you might picture yourself deeply engaged in a creative project and begin taking steps toward making it happen.

The stronger the feeling, the more naturally your actions will align with it. By staying connected to those feelings, you shift your focus, strengthen your motivation, and open yourself to the opportunities and possibilities around you. When you feel it, you start to live it.

The BrainPhone Imagination Flow

Let me guide you through an effective process to energize your imagination by turning on your BrainPhone. Your true feelings are always within you as subtle vibrations, and your BrainPhone helps you tune in to them. But when you're overwhelmed by constant thoughts, emotions, and sensory inputs, it becomes harder to recognize what you're feeling deep down. To reconnect, you need to take a moment to quiet your mind and calm your senses.

The first step is to shift your focus inward, into the present moment—in other words, to turn on your BrainPhone. A simple way to do this is by bringing your attention to your body through gentle movements, as your awareness naturally follows physical sensations.

You'll begin with two light exercises to relax your body and create a steady rhythm. After that, you'll spend a few minutes calming your thoughts and emotions with energy-sensing and breathing techniques. Once you're centered, you'll use your feelings to clarify what you truly want and imagine it happening, allowing those feelings to guide your experience.

Visualization is a form of Brain Sports. It's more than just mental focus—it engages your entire body and mind, connecting your energy to your goals. Like tapping, breathing, or energy-sensing, visualization activates your BrainPhone by aligning your thoughts, emotions, and physical state. With practice, it becomes a powerful skill that grows stronger over time, much like other Brain Sports activities.

The following exercises combine physical movement, energy awareness, and mental focus to create a well-rounded practice. Together, they help you achieve a balanced state where your BrainPhone functions at its best, enhancing your ability to stay focused and turn your aspirations into reality.

FULL-BODY TAPPING

Stand comfortably with your feet shoulder-width apart. If standing isn't comfortable, you can do this while sitting in a chair or on the floor. Relax your wrists, and gently tap your entire head with your fingertips slightly bent. Tap evenly across the top, sides, front, back, forehead, cheeks, chin, and around your ears. As you tap, take deep breaths, exhaling with a soft sigh or sound.

Extend your left arm comfortably in front of you and use the palm of your right hand to rhythmically tap your left shoulder and arm. Focus on the sensations you feel as you tap, imagining the vibrations reaching deep into your body. For added benefit, lightly bounce your knees, creating a gentle, soothing vibration throughout your body. Then, switch hands and tap your right shoulder and arm in the same way.

Next, use one hand to gently tap your chest, starting in the center and gradually moving to the left and right sides. Tap with a smooth, steady rhythm, adjusting your hand position naturally as you go. Keep a light bounce in your knees as you tap. Move down to your lower rib cage and tap evenly from side to side. Then shift to your lower belly, tapping the center first, then the sides, thoroughly covering the whole area.

After that, tap your legs, moving freely. Tap the front, sides, and back of your thighs, including your buttocks. Continue to the lower legs, tapping your calves, ankles, and feet. As you tap, you might feel sensations like tingling, warmth, or slight discomfort in certain areas. Simply notice these sensations while breathing in and out comfortably.

Finally, use both palms or a lightly clenched fist to tap your lower abdomen just below your navel. Keep your arms loose and relaxed, tapping in a steady, rhythmic way. Repeat this focused tapping 100 to 300 times, noticing the warmth and energy spreading through your lower abdomen and lower back.

When you finish, gently place your hands on your lower belly and sweep them clockwise. Take a few deep breaths, focusing on the warmth and calmness in your lower abdomen.

TOE TAPPING

After finishing the Full-Body Tapping exercise, sit comfortably on the floor with your legs stretched out in front of you. Place your hands on the floor behind your hips for support. Keep your legs together, and lightly tap the insides of your feet together, creating a gentle clicking sound. Move your feet quickly and smoothly, letting your big toes touch each other and then letting the pinky toes lightly tap the floor. Keep the movement steady at a pace that feels comfortable for you.

If your hips or lower back feel stiff, this movement might be challenging at first. Don't force it—start with around 30 repetitions and build up gradually. As your body becomes more used to the movement, aim for 100 to 300 repetitions. If you need to, take a short break of 30 seconds to a minute and then try again.

As you do the exercise, breathe in through your nose and out naturally through your mouth, paying attention to the sensations in your body.

ENERGY-SENSING AND BREATHING

After the Toe Tapping exercise, sit comfortably in a chair or on the floor with your back straight but relaxed. If you're sitting in a chair, place the soles of your feet flat on the ground. Raise your hands to chest level, keeping your wrists, fingers, and shoulders relaxed, and lightly tap your fingertips together for one minute.

Then, with your hands still raised, rotate your wrists back and forth quickly for another minute while exhaling through your mouth to release tension.

Now, place your hands a few inches above your knees, palms facing up, with a small gap between your arms and torso so they don't touch. Slowly rotate both hands outward, tracing small circles parallel to the floor, focusing your attention on your palms. You might notice tingling, warmth, a sense of weight, or a subtle pulse—these are energy sensations.

When you feel the energy in your palms, turn your hands so your palms face each other, about two inches apart, and slowly move your palms apart and back together, keeping them close but not touching. Focus on the energy between your hands as you repeat this movement for three to five minutes. As your sensitivity grows, you may feel the energy extend to your arms, as if your hands and arms are surrounded by a warm, invisible layer or moving through water.

Gently bring your hands toward your chest, palms facing it, leaving a small space between your hands and your body. Focus on the warmth and energy from your palms, imagining it seeping into your chest, and feel your chest open and expand as you hold this focus.

Let your hands rest comfortably in your lap and shift your attention to your breathing. Breathe naturally without forcing it. Over time, you'll notice tension in your chest and shoulders easing and your breathing becoming deeper and smoother. As you inhale, feel your chest and belly expand gently, and as you exhale, allow your whole body to relax a little more. In this relaxed state, you may experience a sense of lightness combined with a deep feeling of groundedness in both your body and mind.

As you rest your attention on your chest, you'll notice subtle vibrations and feelings. This is a space where you can reflect on your goals and desires, gaining insights through feelings rather than words. Ask yourself questions like, "Is this what I truly want?" or "What feelings am I hoping to experience with this goal?" Pay attention to how your heart responds—not with words, but with feelings or sensations. Then ask, "What can I do now to move toward this goal?" and let your brain provide the guidance.

EMPOWERING YOUR IMAGINATION WITH FEELING

Continue to breathe naturally and bring the goal you want to achieve into your mind. As you focus, imagine activating the "Imagination" app on your BrainPhone. Picture a large 3D screen in front of you, vivid and lifelike, as if you're stepping into a fully immersive VR movie. See your goal clearly on the screen as a living moment you are experiencing right now.

Engage all your senses to make this moment feel real and alive. Experience the feelings you would have when you achieve your goal, notice the environment around you, hear the sounds, and sense the presence of anyone who is part of this vision. Imagine yourself in this scene, already having achieved your goal and fully experiencing the feelings that come with it.

Let the feeling of accomplishment rise from deep within your chest, whether it's joy, contentment, or peace. Allow this feeling to expand, filling your chest with warmth and spreading throughout your body. In this moment, feel yourself becoming the person who has already achieved the goal.

Raise your hands to chest level, palms facing forward, and gently extend your arms. Imagine the energy and warmth in your chest flowing out through your palms. Picture this energy traveling toward the goal on the screen in front of you, making it feel more real and tangible. As this energy flows, feel a growing sense of clarity and conviction that you have already achieved what you desire.

If some people or circumstances will help you achieve your goal, imagine them appearing on the screen. Send them positive energy and gratitude for their role in your journey. This isn't just a wish; it's a deep, confident acknowledgment that the outcome is already in motion.

Fill your heart with gratitude for what you are visualizing, as if it has already come true. Let this gratitude deepen, lifting your energy and reinforcing your belief in the goal's fulfillment. Feel how this gratitude strengthens and energizes you.

When you're ready, gently lower your hands to your lap and take a few deep breaths. Rub your palms together briskly until they feel warm, then lightly sweep them over your face and body to finish the practice.

* * *

From the Full-Body Tapping exercise to sending energy to your goal, you can take your time with each step to extend the practice to 30 minutes or more, fully immersing yourself in the process. Once familiar with the steps, you can complete the practice effectively in 5–10 minutes.

Every morning and evening, take a moment to turn inward and visualize your goals. In the morning, start by giving thanks for the fresh start of the day and clearly setting your intentions for what you want to accomplish. In the evening, before going to bed, reflect on your goal again and let a sense of gratitude and fulfillment fill your mind and body, imagining your goal as if it's already been achieved. Repeating this simple imagination routine each morning and evening helps align your mind and body, creating a focused energy that naturally attracts the opportunities and people needed to reach your goals.

When you tune in to your inner feelings during this practice, you create a powerful connection between your imagination and your deepest desires. These feelings are at the heart of the energy that links your brain, body, and goals. Focusing your imagination on your inner feelings can transform your mindset, shift your energy, and move you closer to the life you want to create. When you align your imagination with your feelings, you don't just dream of change—you begin to see how to bring it to life. The next step is creativity, where ideas take shape and become reality through intentional action.

CHAPTER 6

RECLAIM YOUR CREATIVITY

Many think creativity is the ability to conceive brilliant ideas, invent revolutionary technologies, or create professional art. They see it as a rare gift reserved for geniuses and uniquely talented individuals, so they believe they are not creative.

But creativity isn't limited to a select few—it's something we all have in abundance. Creativity is a fundamental human trait, an innate quality we're born with. Whether we realize it or not, creativity is present in every aspect of our lives. From how we plan our day, organize our work, and decorate our space to how we connect with others, creativity is woven into everything we do. It shapes even the simplest moments of our lives, making each expression uniquely our own.

While all humans share certain universal traits, we are also distinctly unique. We have different looks, personalities, talents, and unique vibrations that set us apart. Creativity allows us to tap into this uniqueness, express it, and bring it into the world in our own way. To keep creativity alive, you must consciously understand and express your true self. This self-awareness is the foundation for rekindling the creativity that is inherent in all of us.

In nature, every living thing naturally expresses itself. A rose blooms as a rose, and a pine tree grows as a pine tree. The rose doesn't try to grow like a pine tree, and the pine tree doesn't try to bloom like a rose. Similarly, our creativity thrives when we focus on realizing our own potential rather than comparing ourselves to others.

When you activate your BrainPhone, you reconnect with your true self and awaken your natural creativity. It helps you tune in to your inner energy and imagination, bringing your unique vibrations and authenticity into everything you do.

As you embrace your uniqueness, you naturally infuse creativity into your daily activities, turning ordinary tasks into meaningful experiences. Even simple activities like washing dishes, cleaning, or gardening become creative expressions when you approach them with care and intention. It's not just about doing things differently but about doing them with more heart and awareness.

For example, if cleaning the toilet feels dull, humming a tune or smiling while doing it can completely shift the experience. By changing your energy or approach, you turn any task into an act of creation. Brain Sports helps you make creativity an active and intentional part of your life. It demonstrates that reclaiming creativity means transforming everyday actions into meaningful and purposeful expressions, rather than waiting for inspiration to strike. Through exercises that tap into your imagination, improve focus, and find inspiration in daily tasks, Brain Sports helps you naturally integrate creativity into everything you do.

When creativity becomes a natural part of your life, even the most repetitive or mundane tasks take on new meaning and become opportunities for self-expression. Using your BrainPhone in these small moments helps align your thoughts, feelings, and actions, allowing creativity to flow naturally as part of who you are. The focus isn't on achieving something extraordinary but on bringing your unique energy into everything you do and finding joy in the process, no matter how big or small the task.

Natural Brain vs. Cultivated Brain

We're all born with a "natural brain" that imagines and explores freely. This natural brain is inherently curious, full of unconventional thinking, and brimming with creative energy. It allows us to see endless possibilities in the world around us.

As children, our natural brain flourishes. We question and experiment without fear of failure, treating the world like a giant playground. A child can spend hours entertained by just drawing on a piece of paper or watching ants move in and out of their tiny hills. To a child, a pebble becomes a treasure, and an empty box transforms into a castle or spaceship. Everything holds potential, sparking curiosity and endless imagination.

However, as we grow up, this natural creativity often diminishes. Society shapes our natural brains into "cultivated brains" by teaching us rules, standards, and a fear of failure. We begin prioritizing stability and practicality, avoiding risk at all costs. Over time, our thinking becomes automatic, following familiar paths and well-trodden frameworks. Self-doubt creeps in, whispering, "What if I fail?" or "I'm not good enough for that." This shift narrows our focus, turning life into a series of routines and obligations. Instead of enjoying the process, we become fixated on outcomes and performance, seeing failure as something to avoid rather than an opportunity to learn and grow.

Reigniting creativity doesn't mean mastering something entirely new—it's about rediscovering a natural part of yourself that's always been there. It's about reconnecting with your true self and activating your BrainPhone to facilitate that connection. Your BrainPhone helps you tune in to your inner energy and imagination, enabling you to unlock the creative potential that has been within you all along.

How do you connect to your natural brain? The answer is the same—activate your BrainPhone by turning your focus inward. Start noticing what's happening inside—your thoughts, emotions, and feelings. As mentioned in Chapter 4, it's about tuning in to your own vibrations.

Your mind is like an ocean, with waves of thoughts and emotions constantly rising and falling. By observing these movements without judgment, you can gain a clearer understanding of yourself. Beneath these passing waves, you'll find the still and steady presence of your inner feelings—a deep sense of calm and clarity that is always there, untouched by the fluctuations of your mind. This practice helps you discover what excites you, sparks your curiosity, and brings you peace and joy. It also helps you recognize patterns, such as when fear or self-doubt is holding you back, empowering you to break free and move forward.

Creativity flows naturally when you figure out what truly interests you and take steps toward doing things that engage and fulfill you. The spark of creativity reignites when you focus on becoming the person you want to be, not the person others expect you to be. Rediscovering what motivates and excites you can breathe new life into passions that you have set aside or forgotten.

The important thing is to start, no matter how small the step. If you feel like drawing, start by doodling. If you're curious about something new, check out an introductory book or a YouTube tutorial. Creativity begins with simple choices and grows as you reflect on each experience and adjust based on what you learn. This habit creates a cycle of creativity and growth. Over time, even small steps add up to meaningful progress. As you learn and grow, your creativity deepens, expanding with every new endeavor.

True creativity emerges from aligning your choices with your inner feelings and using those experiences to shape a life that feels authentic and fulfilling. By turning on your BrainPhone and tapping into your natural brain, you can make creativity a vibrant part of your daily life.

Imagine with Feelings

Creativity thrives on three interconnected pillars: imagination, focus, and action. Together, they transform ideas into reality, guiding you from inspiration to tangible change.

Imagination is the starting point—it opens the door to new possibilities and helps you approach challenges with curiosity and fresh perspectives. It's the spark that ignites creativity, allowing you to picture what doesn't yet exist. Focus takes this spark and shapes it, giving your ideas clarity and direction. Action, the final pillar, turns those ideas into meaningful outcomes. Without imagination, creativity has no fuel. Without focus and action, it cannot grow into something real.

When you turn on your BrainPhone, you activate your imagination in powerful ways. By tuning in to your inner feelings and desires, your BrainPhone helps you envision what you want with clarity and purpose. It becomes a bridge between your creativity and the steps needed to bring your vision to life.

This process begins by identifying what you truly want—not what society or others suggest, but what feels right for you. As introduced in the previous chapter, this alignment with your inner feelings is key to unlocking your full creative potential. To strengthen your imagination, practice visualizing your goals as if they're already happening. Picture the details, engage your senses, and focus on how achieving those goals would feel. This exercise turns imagination into a powerful tool for growth. The more vividly you imagine your desired outcomes, the more empowered you become to take action.

Your BrainPhone enhances imagination by tapping into a vast pool of knowledge and experiences, both within yourself and the world around you. It's like accessing a limitless database of wisdom whenever you need it. This process often leads to unexpected connections, where seemingly unrelated pieces of information come together in meaningful ways. For example, a childhood memory or a passing comment might suddenly inspire the solution to a current challenge. Your imagination connects the dots, turning these fragments into innovative ideas and approaches.

Set aside just a few minutes each day to engage your BrainPhone using the imagination exercises introduced in the previous chapter. With consistent practice, you can transform imagination into a refined skill. Paired with focus and action, it becomes a powerful force, enabling you to bring even your boldest ideas to life.

BRAINPHONE WISDOM MEDITATION

Imagination is a powerful gateway to creativity, especially when combined with practices that deepen your connection to inner wisdom and intuition. One such practice is BrainPhone Wisdom Meditation, which uses the power of imagination to unlock clarity and guidance. By actively engaging with your BrainPhone, you can connect with deeper insights and uncover solutions that feel both meaningful and aligned with your true self. You can turn to it whenever you're seeking inspiration for a problem or clarity regarding a difficult decision.

Start the meditation by calming your mind and turning your focus inward. Think about the problem you want to solve or the decision you're facing. Sometimes, simply sitting with your thoughts this way will bring clarity or an answer. But if you still feel stuck, you can take it further by imagining a conversation with a wise being on your BrainPhone.

This wise being could take many forms. It might be your true self—a version of you that feels wiser and more confident than you are today. It could also be a figure that symbolizes creativity and insight, like a mentor, a loved one, or even a historical figure renowned in a specific field. For example, if your question relates to science, you might imagine connecting to someone like Einstein. For music, perhaps you'd see Mozart. If you're drawn to fictional characters, you might picture Yoda, Gandalf, or anyone who represents wisdom and guidance.

To begin the conversation, take a moment to visualize activating your BrainPhone. Imagine calling the wise being you chose, and hear the subtle sound of the phone ringing. Feel the connection forming in your mind. Then, picture them answering with a warm, welcoming voice, radiating a genuine delight to connect with you and a readiness to offer their guidance.

Their presence becomes vivid—perhaps you see their image appear clearly in your mind's eye or focus on the sound of their voice resonating deeply. As you begin to share your problem, allow yourself to feel completely at ease, as if you're speaking with someone who understands and supports you unconditionally. If you're alone, you might try having the conversation aloud, letting the words flow naturally.

Visualize them listening intently, fully focusing on you, and offering thoughtful advice. This advice may come as clear words, a reassuring feeling, or even a sudden clarity. Whatever form it takes, let it fill you with confidence and provide a sense of direction. Trust in the process and allow their guidance to help you see the path forward.

Although this meditation might feel like receiving guidance from an external source, the wise being is simply a tool to help you access your own intuition. When you turn on your

BrainPhone, you connect with the inner wisdom already within you, uncovering insights and solutions waiting to be found. This practice reminds you that the answers lie within—you just need a moment of quiet focus to hear them.

Sustain Your Focus

Creativity begins with free and flexible thinking, but it takes focus to turn initial ideas into something real and actionable. Inspiration often comes in quick, fleeting bursts, but without sustained concentration, those ideas can fade before they have a chance to grow. Focus helps you stay on course, providing clarity and direction even when distractions or challenges arise.

This is where your BrainPhone makes a difference. By activating it, you redirect your attention inward, away from external noise and toward what truly matters. It helps you tune in to your goals, prioritize your efforts, and channel your energy in to meaningful action.

Focus is the second pillar of creativity, following imagination. It's the essential tool that bridges the gap between envisioning possibilities and making them a reality. I'll now introduce a few Brain Sports practices to help you strengthen your focus power.

RELAXED CONCENTRATION

We're often tense when we concentrate and distracted when we relax, but it's possible to find a balance in a state of "relaxed concentration." This state of mind is when you can deeply focus on something while keeping your body and mind at ease. In this state, your concentration becomes more steady and natural, allowing you to stay focused longer without feeling drained.

When we concentrate, it's often mixed with tension, pressure to perform, or fear of failure. These emotions can make it hard to stay fully present and engaged. Relaxed concentration, on the other hand, clears your mind of unnecessary clutter, making it easier to focus calmly and steadily.

One effective way to practice relaxed concentration is to pay attention to the subtle energy in your body. As you relax and notice sensations like warmth, tingling, or vibration, your body naturally calms, and your focus sharpens. These sensations help you stay grounded and steady while maintaining a sense of inner stability. For a guided practice of sensing energy, see page 80.

Breathing meditation is another simple but powerful method to improve concentration. To begin, sit in a chair or on the floor with your back straight but comfortable. Relax your shoulders and neck, and let your hands rest naturally in your lap. Close your eyes lightly, or keep them half-open. Shift your focus to your breath, inhaling slowly and deeply through your nose and exhaling gently through your mouth. Pay attention to the sensation of the air moving in and out of your lungs. Don't force or control your breathing; instead, allow it to settle into a natural, easy rhythm while keeping your attention on it.

As you focus, notice the sensations of your breath—the air passing through your nostrils or the gentle rise and fall of your chest and stomach. If your mind starts to wander or distractions arise, let those thoughts pass without holding on to them or pushing them away. Each time your attention drifts, gently bring it back to your breath. This practice not only calms your mind but also helps you develop the ability to focus more consistently.

Once you feel comfortable focusing on your breath, you can add a layer of challenge by counting your breaths. Count one inhalation and exhalation cycle as one breath, and continue counting without losing focus. At first, reaching 10 or 20 breaths might be hard without losing track of the count, which is normal. Start small, aiming for 10 or 20, and gradually increase to 30, 50, or even 100 breaths as you improve.

Counting up to 100 breaths in a single, uninterrupted session is a great way to train your concentration. It usually takes 10 to 20 minutes, depending on the pace of your breathing. This exercise is both challenging and rewarding, as it helps you tune out distractions and deepen your focus. Gradually, you'll find that this relaxed concentration becomes easier and helps bring a sense of calm and clarity into your life.

TURN ON YOUR BRAINPHONE'S FOCUS MODE

Concentration isn't just about keeping your attention on a task—it's also about blocking distractions, whether from the outside world or your wandering thoughts. Reducing these distractions allows you to stay in the flow and focus on what matters. If you find it difficult to concentrate because of distractions or internal chatter, try using your BrainPhone's focus mode to refocus your mind.

Think of it like silencing notifications on your phone when you need to focus. Start by imagining activating your BrainPhone and setting it to focus mode. When distractions arise, visualize turning them off, just as you would swipe away a notification or mute an alert. For example, when your mind starts to wander, imagine pressing a mental "focus" button, swiping a distraction away, or saying "stop" or "off" out loud. These simple actions signal to your brain that it's time to concentrate, helping you filter out distractions and stay on task.

Another helpful technique is to work in focused intervals, setting a timer for a specific amount of time—such as 20 or 30 minutes—and committing to a single task during that period. Once the timer goes off, take a short break to refresh your mind before starting the next session. Pairing this structured approach with your BrainPhone's focus mode can reinforce your ability to concentrate and make it easier to block out interruptions.

By visualizing and activating your BrainPhone's focus mode, you train your mind to enter a state of deep concentration more effectively. This practice strengthens your ability to stay focused, reduces distractions, and creates an environment where you can work with greater clarity and purpose.

Take Action Persistently

Creativity isn't just about generating ideas—it's about bringing them to life. Ideas, no matter how brilliant, hold no value if they remain in our minds. Action is what transforms imagination into reality and turns thoughts into tangible results.

By taking consistent, deliberate steps, we breathe life into our ideas and move closer to our goals. Action doesn't require perfection; it requires persistence and a willingness to learn and adapt along the way. This is how we create—not just by envisioning possibilities, but by committing to the process of making them real.

THE POWER OF GRIT AND PERSISTENCE

In an ancient Chinese tale, a 90-year-old man lived with two massive mountains blocking his house, forcing him to take a long detour every time he traveled. One day, he made a bold decision—he resolved to move the mountains and level the ground near his home. He and his descendants began digging the next day, carrying the dirt and stones to a distant sea.

Observing their effort, a friend scoffed and said, "You'll never live long enough to move those mountains. How could you possibly finish such a huge task?" The old man replied calmly, "Even if I don't finish, my descendants will carry on. Our hands won't stop working, and the mountains won't grow any bigger. One day, we will move them."

Inspired by his determination, others joined in. Their persistence and hard work paid off when, moved by their effort, the gods shifted both mountains overnight. Finally, a clear, flat road stretched in front of his house.

Similarly, the Indigenous people of North America used the power of persistence. During droughts, tribes would gather to dance, pray, and celebrate a powwow. When they danced together, rain would always come. When a young man asked an elder how they made it happen, the elder replied, "We dance until it rains."

Achieving anything comes down to sticking with it—to the belief that if you keep going, you can move a mountain and make the rains come when they are most needed. The steady, consistent effort brings results.

Angela Duckworth, an American psychologist, is known for her research on grit. She describes grit as a combination of "passion" and "perseverance" toward a long-term goal. Grit is not simply endurance, which is the ability to keep doing the same thing for a long time. Instead, it's the strength to pursue a clear goal while believing in your growth along the way.

People with grit are self-motivated and follow through, even when they don't get recognition from others. Duckworth found that grit matters more for success than talent or IQ. Talent alone doesn't guarantee long-term success. People with grit don't quit when they face difficulties and setbacks. In fact, the tougher the challenge, the more determined they become.

Neuroscientists say persistence and grit are essential for making changes in the brain that enhance problem-solving and emotional resilience. While mindless repetition can lead to boredom, goal-driven repetition fueled by grit strengthens neural connections. These pathways make your brain more efficient, boosting its ability to learn, solve problems, and handle change.

Grit and persistence also activate the brain's reward system, releasing dopamine—a chemical that creates feelings of pleasure and motivation. The key isn't just enduring repetition; it is having a clear, meaningful goal and the confidence that you're making progress. This sense of purpose triggers dopamine release, fueling a feeling of accomplishment and driving the motivation to keep moving forward.

Tasks that require grit and persistence can be challenging, putting stress on both body and mind. But not all stress is bad. When managed well, repeated exposure to challenges trains your brain to adapt, building resilience over time. As you overcome obstacles, your brain becomes more efficient and better equipped to tackle future challenges confidently and effectively.

Set goals, stay motivated, and approach them with grit and persistence. These efforts strengthen your brain, building the resilience and capability needed to achieve your goals

REDISCOVERING YOUR INNER GRIT

If you've ever doubted whether you have the grit and persistence to succeed, take a moment to think back to when you were a toddler. Most babies start walking between 9 and 18 months of age. The process involves constant trying and falling. Babies attempt to stand dozens of times a day, repeating this for weeks and months until, after around 1,000 attempts, they succeed in walking.

Nearly all humans accomplish this challenging feat, yet we forget that it's a powerful example of grit. As babies, we set a goal—to walk—and didn't stop until we achieved it. Each slight improvement motivated us to try again, often with the support and encouragement of those around us. Along the way, we learned to walk and developed skills like patience, self-regulation, and the ability to learn through trial and error.

You don't lack persistence. Think about how you learned to speak, write, tie your shoes, or drive a car—it took countless tries and challenges to master these basic skills. The problem isn't a lack of persistence but how modern life, with its fast pace and instant gratification, makes it harder to fully harness the strength you already have.

When pursuing a goal, don't measure success or failure too soon. Grit and persistence aren't about avoiding failure but about continuing despite it. Like when you learned to walk, it's about getting back up each time you fall. Grit and persistence have the power to make the impossible possible. They transform dreams into achievements, obstacles into opportunities, and ordinary efforts into extraordinary success stories.

Don't Worry Too Much about "Why" and "How"

When we decide to do something, it's easy to get stuck asking, "Why?" and "How?" These questions can lead to overthinking and overanalyzing, making it harder to take action.

We often ask why to justify our choices, sometimes to others and ourselves. But when we really want something or feel strongly about it, we don't stop to ask why—we just act. Neuroscientist Antonio Damasio found that our answers to why often come after the fact—they're logical explanations for decisions we've already made based on feelings.

When making big decisions that affect others, having a rational why might be necessary. But for personal choices, sometimes wanting something sincerely is reason enough to act. Overthinking why often leads to hesitation and procrastination, draining the energy and excitement to act.

The same goes for how. Life's most important skills and experiences rarely come from having everything figured out in advance. When you first learned to walk, you didn't know how—you just tried until you succeeded.

Instead of overthinking, start small. Begin with what you can do. As you act, the why will become clearer, and the how will emerge through experience. Let go of the need for perfect answers and take the first step with curiosity and excitement.

Internal Integration

So far, we've explored the three pillars of creativity—imagination, focus, and action—and how the BrainPhone can help you strengthen each. Equally important, however, is achieving internal integration: the alignment of your thoughts, feelings, and actions. This alignment is essential for unlocking your full creative potential and living authentically.

Have you ever considered how much alignment exists between what you think you should do, how you feel about it, and what you actually do? The results of your efforts often hinge on whether these three parts are working together or pulling in different directions. For example, you might decide to exercise every morning to stay healthy, but when the alarm goes off, you feel tired and unmotivated. Instead of putting on your workout clothes and starting your day, you stay in bed or watch TV. This mismatch between thought, feeling, and action leaves you frustrated and disappointed.

When your thoughts, feelings, and actions are misaligned, your energy becomes scattered. It's like a carriage being pulled in different directions by three horses—progress becomes slow, difficult, and draining. This lack of coordination not only wastes energy but also creates internal conflict, adding stress and frustration to your life.

However, when your thoughts, feelings, and actions align, your energy becomes focused and balanced. This harmony creates inner stability, authenticity, and clarity, empowering you to move toward your goals with purpose. In this state of alignment, you unlock your ability to create meaningful change, achieve your dreams, and live a life that truly reflects who you are.

Everything in the world, including your brain, heart, and body, carries a unique vibration. When your thoughts, feelings, and actions are out of sync, these vibrations clash, creating internal dissonance. This dissonance leaves you feeling confused, frustrated, and disconnected. Over time, it erodes your self-esteem and diminishes your sense of purpose.

For example, internal conflict grows when you deeply desire something but deny it out of fear. Your brain may push you to move forward, but your heart holds back with anxiety, and your body resists taking action. This misalignment not only creates confusion within but also sends mixed signals to those around you. Even the universe, which responds to clear intentions, cannot fully support you if it doesn't understand what you truly want.

To unlock the creative energy of your brain, harmonize your thoughts, feelings, and actions. Aligning these three brings the vibrations of your brain, heart, and body into sync, creating a powerful force for transformation.

The first step toward this integration is discovering what you truly want—not what you think you should want or feel pressured to pursue. Use the BrainPhone to listen to your inner feelings, identify your authentic desires, and take actions that resonate with them. Practicing Brain Sports can further enhance this process by helping you cultivate focus and presence, grounding your energy and amplifying your intentions.

Often, people lose direction or give up on their goals, not because circumstances are too challenging, but because they've disconnected from the feeling that first inspired them. What we call "lost motivation" or "waning interest" is often a loss of connection to that initial spark. Staying connected to this feeling, even during tough times, provides the resilience and energy to keep moving forward.

When your thoughts, feelings, and actions align, you create a sense of harmony that connects your values to how you live. This alignment brings authenticity and consistency to your life, helping you feel more grounded and true to yourself. Authenticity builds self-trust, confidence, and respect, empowering you to break free from old habits, discover hidden strengths, and shape a life that reflects your true goals and desires. By activating the BrainPhone and practicing Brain Sports, you can develop this alignment and unlock the full potential of your creativity.

CHAPTER 7

LIFT YOUR LIFE WITH BRAIN PULL-UPS

We've seen how imagination, focus, and action, guided by the BrainPhone, unlock your mind's potential to create meaningful change. Yet, true transformation involves more than the mind—it requires a deep connection between the mind and body. Physical challenges are one of the most powerful ways to activate this connection. This is where Brain Sports shine, combining physical effort with mental focus to support meaningful and lasting growth.

Physical challenges are unique because they provide concrete, undeniable evidence of change. When you set a goal and work steadily toward it, your body adapts, and your brain recognizes the progress. This builds trust in yourself, reinforcing the belief that growth is possible. Feeling your muscles grow stronger or your endurance improve creates a feedback loop of motivation and confidence, reminding you that consistent effort leads to extraordinary results.

The key is to set a goal that is challenging enough to surprise your brain—one that pushes your limits without overwhelming you and feels achievable with persistence and effort. A good challenge engages your brain, encourages commitment, and provides opportunities for growth every step of the way.

For example, if you don't usually run, you might train for a 5K. If you're new to fitness, you could work toward completing 10, 20, or even 50 push-ups over time. Or, you might try something entirely new, like learning qigong or martial arts, mastering movements that feel difficult at first but become natural with practice.

Among these challenges, pull-ups stand out as one of the most effective and transformative exercises. They are a great example of Brain Sports, combining physical strength with mental discipline. It may seem unusual for a meditation expert to suggest pull-ups, but my focus has always been on brain training—and pull-ups are a powerful tool for this purpose. Meditation unlocks your brain's potential in one way, while pull-ups do so in another, equally valuable way.

Pull-ups may seem like a simple fitness exercise. However, they represent the persistence, resilience, and self-transformation explored throughout this book. Working toward your first pull-up—or increasing your count—isn't just about physical strength. It's a holistic process that strengthens your body, sharpens your mind, and builds your spirit.

By integrating pull-ups into your Brain Sports practice, you'll experience firsthand how aligning your mind and body can transform not only your physical abilities but also your perspective on what you can achieve. This exercise builds self-trust, boosts motivation, and demonstrates how consistent effort can lead to meaningful change in every area of your life.

My Pull-Up Story

I've been practicing martial arts, like Tae Kwon Do and Aikido, since I was a teenager, so staying active has always been a part of my life. When I was younger, doing pull-ups felt natural—something I didn't even think twice about. Over the years, my focus shifted to other forms of exercise and meditation, and I didn't do pull-ups for decades. Then, two years ago, at age 72, I saw some of my students doing pull-ups and thought, *Why not give it another try?*

To my surprise, I couldn't even lift myself off the ground. My arms barely bent, and just hanging from the bar felt like a struggle. My hands and arms ached, and I thought, *Wow, this is much harder than I expected.* It was a humbling moment, realizing how much my strength had diminished despite staying active all these years.

But I didn't let that stop me. I set a goal to do pull-ups again and started small. I installed a bar above a door in my home and made it a habit to hang from it whenever I walked by. Whether going to the bathroom, getting a cup of water, or moving around the house, I stopped to practice. I also added exercises like push-ups, sit-ups, dumbbell curls, and weight training to build strength in my arms, back, and core. It wasn't easy—my palms blistered and callused—but I kept going.

After months of relentless practice, the moment finally came. With every ounce of strength and determination, I pulled myself up. My chin crossed the bar, and then, finally, my chest pressed against it. For a brief second, time seemed to stand still. The joy I felt at that moment was indescribable. It wasn't just about gaining strength—it was about the deep fulfillment of persevering through something difficult and achieving it. At that moment, I felt unstoppable, and I wanted everyone to experience the incredible triumph of overcoming something difficult.

Pull-ups have become more than an exercise for me—they reflect a journey of growth and purpose. At 67, I launched a project in New Zealand called Earth Village, a space where young people from around the world come together to train their minds and bodies, develop leadership skills, and learn how to live in harmony with others and nature. Around that time, I also wrote *I've Decided to Live 120 Years* as a personal commitment to see Earth Village thrive and to inspire others to embrace the second half of life with vibrancy and meaning.

In the book, I shared my philosophy: "Physical power is life—just move, no matter what." Pull-ups became a way to put this belief into action and prove it to myself. They also demonstrated my conviction that consistent effort always pays off. Today, pull-ups are a daily ritual for me, reaffirming my commitment to keep moving forward. They have become a grounding practice as essential as meditation, providing discipline, focus, and a renewed sense of purpose.

Why Pull-Ups Activate Your BrainPhone

Pull-ups are one of the most effective exercises for building full-body strength. They work your arms, shoulders, back, and chest muscles, especially targeting your back and arms. They also engage your core, helping improve balance and stability. With regular practice, pull-ups can boost endurance, support fat loss, and improve your overall fitness and body shape.

Despite these benefits, pull-ups might not seem like the most obvious choice for general health. However, I recommend them for their unique ability to powerfully activate your BrainPhone.

What sets pull-ups apart is their clarity and honesty. The goal is straightforward: if your chin clears the bar, you succeed; if it doesn't, you don't. This simplicity is highly motivating. Each successful pull-up delivers a sense of achievement, building confidence and self-trust. These small wins accumulate, inspiring you to take on greater challenges. There are no gimmicks or shortcuts. You can't accidentally do a pull-up or fake your way through it. They require consistent effort and real progress. That's why succeeding feels so rewarding.

Pull-ups aren't easy, which is precisely why they're so valuable. Lifting your body weight challenges your physical limits, demanding focus and discipline. While goals like walking 10,000 steps or doing a few sets of push-ups are manageable for most, pull-ups push you further, making them a true test of strength and resilience.

Our bodies and minds hold untapped potential. The upper body strength our ancestors used to climb and navigate their environment is still within us, even if modern life has dulled these abilities. With practice, you can reclaim this strength and agility. Achieving pull-ups requires persistence and the willingness to face setbacks, but every attempt builds resilience. When you finally succeed, it's about more than completing a pull-up—it's about proving to yourself that you can overcome challenges once thought impossible.

Pull-ups also strengthen the connection between your body and brain. This exercise demands your brain to coordinate your entire body, not just your arms and back. Your core stabilizes, your legs assist with balance, and your brain fine-tunes every movement. This integration enhances brain function by sharpening neural pathways, and improving physical control, focus, and precision. Pull-ups are not just a strength exercise—they train your brain to work more effectively with your body.

Most importantly, pull-ups change your brain. The process of learning and practicing pull-ups stimulates neuroplasticity. Challenging exercises like pull-ups push your brain to adapt by forming new neural connections. As you continue, what once seemed impossible becomes achievable.

Failure is an essential part of this transformation. Each attempt, successful or not, helps your brain identify limitations, develop solutions, and strengthen neural connections. This process builds not only physical ability but also persistence, discipline, and self-control.

When you take on pull-ups with a clear goal, you train yourself to stay focused on long-term progress, strengthen control over your body and mind, and build the resilience to overcome setbacks. These mental and physical gains foster a growth-oriented mindset that extends far beyond exercise, empowering success in all areas of life.

An 84-Year-Old's Pull-Ups

After experiencing how pull-ups can transform body and mind, I became passionate about them as a powerful Brain Sports activity. I began recommending pull-ups to others, researching ways to make them more accessible, and encouraging people to take on the challenge. In the fall of 2024, I helped organize a pull-up challenge competition in South Korea that brought together people from all backgrounds to celebrate their hard work and dedication.

One of the most inspiring participants was Jungin, an 84-year-old woman who received a special award as the oldest competitor. She amazed everyone by completing eight pull-ups. With her lean, athletic frame, graying hair, and strikingly toned muscles, she displayed incredible strength and determination. "I've been practicing pull-ups for 10 years, little by little," she shared. "There were times I wanted to quit when it didn't go well, but as my health improved and others encouraged me, I felt proud and kept going."

Jungin had begun working out every morning at dawn in her local park and eventually decided to try pull-ups. Her steady commitment paid off, and her progress didn't go unnoticed. Watching her practice, some older women in the neighborhood felt inspired and began joining her. "They used to tell me they felt weak and unwell," she shared with a proud smile, "but now they say they feel stronger and healthier—and they credit me for it." She now has her sights set on achieving 15 pull-ups next year.

Most participants in the competition weren't skilled at pull-ups when they began. One young competitor, who had been bullied in middle school for his small, weak frame, discovered street workouts—a form of calisthenics performed in public spaces. He didn't just master traditional pull-ups; he transformed them into fluid, acrobatic movements that made him appear to fly on the bars, earning cheers and admiration from the audience.

For every participant, pull-ups became more than just an exercise—they became a means of growth. Through repeated effort, they pushed past their limits and replaced the "I can't" mindset with a strong sense of "I can." The competition highlighted how something as simple as a pull-up bar can inspire resilience, determination, and meaningful change.

How Pull-Ups Build Your Mind

Many people feel frustrated when they first try pull-ups. No matter how hard you pull, your body doesn't move, and your brain quickly concludes, "I can't do this." It's tempting to rationalize, "Why bother with something so hard? It's not going to change my life if I don't."

We tend to avoid hard things, choosing what feels easy and comfortable in the moment, believing that's the path to happiness. But true growth comes from stepping out of that comfort zone and facing challenges head-on. Saying, "I can only do what I can do," keeps you stuck, preventing you from exploring your full potential.

While there's a certain joy in comfort and familiarity, there's a deeper, more lasting joy in accomplishing something you once thought impossible. Completing your first pull-up is a gratifying experience. It's not about recognition or rewards from others—it's the quiet satisfaction of knowing you've achieved something through your own hard work. That sense of accomplishment builds trust and confidence in your ability to tackle new challenges.

For someone who can't yet do a pull-up, the initial reaction might be, "This is too hard. It hurts. I can't do this." These thoughts and feelings are natural, instinctive responses from your body and mind. But choosing to push forward despite them can transform your reality. By deciding to "do it anyway," you quiet negative thoughts, awaken your mind, and re-energize your brain. This is the power of the BrainPhone in action—an awakened mind overcoming limits. Pull-ups challenge and strengthen this mental power, which is why I call them Brain Pull-ups.

Age or weight doesn't have to make pull-ups unattainable. Yes, they're challenging, especially for those in their 40s, 50s, and beyond. Likely, fewer than 5 percent of people over 40 can do a pull-up. But with consistent training, they're possible—even into your 70s or beyond.

As we age, it's normal for muscle mass to decline, starting in our 30s and 40s and accelerating in our 60s. By your 60s, you might have lost about 30 percent of your muscle mass; by your 80s, it could be closer to 50 percent. The good news is that strength training can slow or even reverse this process. Consistent effort rebuilds lost muscle and keeps your body strong. For example, the

84-year-old woman I mentioned earlier started practicing pull-ups in her mid-70s and succeeded through steady, focused effort.

Taking on pull-ups later in life is a significant challenge, but even attempting them is worthwhile. When I got into pull-ups, I discovered countless inspiring videos online. People who were overweight or had never exercised before documented their journey toward completing a single pull-up. Watching them struggle, push through setbacks, and finally succeed—sometimes after months or even years—was a powerful reminder of what's possible. Their stories show that anyone can achieve what once seemed impossible with consistent effort and determination.

Lift Your Body, Lift Your Life

When doubt clouds your path or your confidence wavers, pull-ups offer a surprising way to restore clarity, rebuild resilience, and reignite your inner drive. While they may seem like a simple physical challenge, their impact goes far deeper, helping you reconnect with your determination and uncover hidden strengths.

Pull-ups require more than physical effort—they demand focus, perseverance, and a willingness to push past discomfort. Each attempt challenges not only your body but also your mind. With every pull, you confront the doubts and fears that weigh you down, transforming them into the strength to rise above.

As you lift yourself higher, pull-ups become a metaphor for overcoming life's obstacles. The bar represents a threshold—a division between the world of limitations below and the world of possibilities above. Below the bar lie fears, doubts, and excuses that hold you back. But as you pull yourself up, you rise into a space of confidence, fulfillment, and new perspectives. The moment your chin clears the bar is a reminder that perseverance can turn the seemingly impossible into an empowering reality.

This process isn't just about building physical strength. Pull-ups help release mental and emotional burdens like anxiety, stress, and self-doubt. With each pull, you let go of patterns and behaviors that no longer serve you. With consistent effort, this practice cultivates a sense of balance and freedom, lightening both body and mind.

Even if you've never done a pull-up, setting a goal to achieve one can be transformative. It's not focused on being perfect or competing with others—it's about committing to yourself and taking small, steady steps to grow. Each attempt strengthens not only your muscles but also your resolve, helping you build the discipline to overcome challenges in all areas of life.

So, tell yourself, "I'm going to lift my body," or even, "I'll do one pull-up before I die." With every pull, you're not just lifting your body—you're lifting your life. Pull-ups are a surprising yet powerful way to rediscover your strength, renew your energy, and create a life rooted in purpose and resilience.

Tips for Brain Pull-Ups

Whether you're starting from scratch or looking to improve, pull-ups can feel like a tough challenge. If you've never done one before, set a simple goal: achieve your first pull-up. Give yourself a realistic timeline and focus on making incremental, steady progress. If you're already capable of pull-ups, challenge yourself to aim higher—perhaps double or even triple your current number.

Here are practical tips to help you build strength, stay motivated, and activate your BrainPhone as you work steadily toward your pull-up goal.

TAKE YOUR TIME, DON'T RUSH

If you're new to pull-ups, taking it slow and going at your own pace is important. For example, if you can't even hang from the bar for a second, start there. That's the perfect first step. Don't overdo it. Focus on small, manageable steps and gradually build up your strength.

For those with a basic fitness level, it's possible to complete a single pull-up after two to three months of consistent training. However, if your arms or core strength is weak, starting with foundational exercises like sit-ups and push-ups is best to build strength first. Since pull-ups require multiple upper body muscles working together, attempting them without enough strength can increase the risk of injury.

To prepare for pull-ups, focus on strengthening your chest, core, and back muscles. For chest strength, push-ups are an excellent exercise. If standard push-ups feel too challenging, you can start with knee or wall push-ups and gradually progress to incline or full push-ups as you gain strength. To build core strength, incorporate planks and the Superman pose into your routine. Planks help improve core stability, while the Superman pose targets your core, back, and lower back muscles by lifting your arms and legs simultaneously while lying on your stomach.

For back strength, consider using a weighted exercise machine that allows you to pull your arms toward your body. Start with a manageable weight, such as one-fifth to one-quarter of your body weight, or choose a level that feels challenging but safe. Gradually increase the weight as your strength improves to build the foundation needed for pull-ups.

The key is to respect your body and take a gradual approach. Pull-ups are achievable for anyone willing to focus on steady progress. Avoid rushing, enjoy the process, and maintain a balanced connection between your mind and body as you work toward your goal.

USE YOUR IMAGINATION

Don't rely solely on physical training—use the power of your imagination and activate your BrainPhone to accelerate your progress. Spend time vividly visualizing each step of your movements, as this mental rehearsal has been shown to enhance muscle memory and improve actual performance.

Before each attempt, take a moment to activate your BrainPhone and vividly imagine yourself achieving your pull-up goals. Picture your hands gripping the bar securely, your body rising smoothly, and the sense of accomplishment as you reach the top. This mental rehearsal helps your brain process and internalize the movement. With practice, the action feels more familiar and achievable.

Additionally, incorporate small physical actions during visualization, like squeezing your fists or engaging your core muscles. These simple movements help bridge the gap between mental imagery and physical execution, making the practice more effective and connected to real actions.

Even if you can't do a pull-up yet, visualizing success trains your mind to interpret the action as possible. This practice strengthens the coordination between your brain and body, builds focus, and increases confidence. By engaging your imagination this way, you turn visualization into a powerful tool for steady progress and tangible results.

FOCUS ON PROGRESS, NOT DIFFICULTY

Maintaining a positive and cheerful mindset is essential when practicing pull-ups. Approach each session with optimism and a lighthearted attitude. Instead of fixating on how hard it feels, focus on doing your best and finishing your practice with a sense of accomplishment.

Track small improvements in your strength and ability over time. These incremental changes matter. For instance, if you started struggling just to hang from the bar, perhaps now you can hold on longer or begin to pull yourself up slightly. Even if you haven't completed a full pull-up yet, your body is growing stronger, and your brain is starting to believe in your ability to succeed.

Remember that progress is not always linear. Some days will feel harder than others, but each attempt strengthens your resilience and keeps you moving forward. On tougher days, be kind to yourself and focus on showing up—consistency is what drives growth over time.

Focusing on progress helps keep you motivated and consistent. When you tell yourself, "I can do this," and genuinely believe it, it becomes easier to keep going. Celebrate small victories, stay positive, and allow yourself the time and space to improve. Every step forward is worth it.

By combining physical effort with visualization and a progress-focused mindset, you'll build the strength and confidence needed to achieve your pull-up goals—and discover your true potential in the process.

CHAPTER 8

EXERCISE TO TRANSFORM YOUR LIFE

Pull-ups have shown us how a single physical challenge can strengthen the connection between the mind and body, fostering resilience, focus, and self-trust. They are a powerful example of how consistent effort can unlock potential and lead to meaningful growth. Yet, pull-ups represent just one form of exercise that bridges this connection. Now, we'll expand the focus to exercise as a broader practice—one that everyone can engage in to transform not only their body but also their brain and life.

Exercise is the most accessible and universal Brain Sport—a cornerstone of physical and mental well-being. Among the many ways to activate your body and mind, exercise is the one nearly everyone can relate to and incorporate into daily life. From walking to strength training, it provides a direct path to greater vitality, emotional resilience, and cognitive sharpness.

Exercise isn't just about staying healthy; it's one of the most powerful tools to transform your body, brain, and life. While physical strength brings to mind strong muscles, sturdy bones, and a healthy heart, it's also about fueling the brain. Fitness provides the energy and resources your brain needs to perform at its best. When we're out of shape, it's not just our bodies that suffer—our emotions, intellect, and even character are impacted.

The brain, though only 2 percent of body weight, consumes about 20 percent of total energy. A fit body supports efficient delivery of oxygen and nutrients to the brain, enhancing focus, memory, and problem-solving. Conversely, a lack of fitness diminishes the brain's energy supply, reducing cognitive function and mental performance.

We've all felt it—when we're tired, small irritations magnify, and connecting with others feels harder. This lack of energy impacts our relationships and overall quality of life. Physical fitness supports emotional resilience, social harmony, and brain power. It sustains us as an essential part of living fully as human beings.

Yet many people don't get enough exercise. A 2023 study in the *European Heart Journal* looked at data from over 15,000 people across six studies. It found that participants spent an average of 10.4 hours a day sitting, based on activity monitors worn on their thighs. Americans are sitting more now than ever before. The American Heart Association reports that sedentary jobs have increased by 83 percent since 1950. Johns Hopkins University adds that less than 20 percent of jobs today are physically active, compared to nearly half in 1960.

Dr. James Levine of the Mayo Clinic has famously called prolonged sitting "Sitting Disease," warning of its severe and far-reaching health impacts: "Sitting is more dangerous than smoking, and it kills more people than AIDS." Sedentary behavior is linked to over 30 serious health conditions, including obesity, cardiovascular disease, and diabetes.

Prolonged sitting doesn't just harm your body—it also damages brain health. Inactivity limits oxygen and nutrient supply to the brain, impairing focus, memory, and flexibility while increasing stress, depression, and cognitive decline.

Fortunately, even modest physical activity can revitalize brain energy. Simple actions like light cardio, standing up, or taking a few steps can deliver immediate benefits. That's why exercise is widely regarded as one of the most effective tools for maintaining brain health. By integrating even small movements into your day, you can unlock your body and brain's potential for growth, vitality, and resilience.

Exercise Makes You Feel Better

One of the most immediate effects of exercise on the brain is its ability to enhance your mood. During physical activity, the brain releases neurotransmitters like serotonin, which fosters a sense of calmness and happiness; dopamine, which boosts motivation and pleasure; endorphins, which alleviate pain and fatigue and create a feeling of exhilaration; and endocannabinoids, which help reduce stress and promote relaxation.

These chemical reactions contribute to the well-known phenomenon of "runner's high," often experienced during exercise. The runner's high is a state of euphoria and lightness that typically begins about 30 minutes into a workout, when fatigue fades, movements feel more fluid, and a sense of renewal takes over. While it is commonly associated with running, this sensation can also occur during other prolonged activities such as swimming, cycling, and skiing or team sports like soccer, baseball, and rugby.

Even when a runner's high is not achieved, exercise still has a remarkable ability to uplift your mood and improve mental well-being. The mental health benefits of physical activity are widely recognized. In 2010, researchers from the University of Vermont studied the effects of exercise on mood in adults aged 18–25. Participants who rode an indoor bike for 20 minutes reported feeling better afterward, with these positive effects lasting for up to 12 hours.

Further evidence of exercise's impact on mental health comes from a 2019 study conducted by researchers at the Harvard T.H. Chan School of Public Health. Analyzing the health records and genetic data of nearly 8,000 people, they found that regular physical activity significantly reduces the risk of depression. This benefit was observed not only in vigorous workouts but also in lighter forms of exercise such as yoga or aerobics. The study concluded that as little as 35 minutes of daily exercise can lower the risk of depression. Adding up to four hours of exercise per week can further reduce the risk by as much as 17 percent.

In 2022, an Austrian study suggested that exercise could be even more effective than traditional treatments like psychotherapy or medication for certain mental health issues. The research highlighted the effectiveness of short, intense workouts, which were found to be 1.5 times more effective than medication or cognitive behavioral therapy in alleviating mild depression, stress, and anxiety. Dr. Ben Singh, who led the study, emphasized that exercise should be considered a key treatment option for improving mental health.

The evidence is clear: all forms of exercise are effective tools for improving mental well-being. Beyond enhancing physical fitness, exercise has a meaningful impact on mood, reduces stress, and builds resilience against mental health challenges like depression and anxiety. It's one of the best investments you can make for the health of your brain, mind, and body.

Exercise Makes You Smarter

Exercise not only makes you feel good, but it also improves your brain's ability to think, remember, and learn. A growing body of research shows that regular exercise activates and strengthens key areas of the brain involved in cognitive processes.

One of the most critical areas affected by exercise is the hippocampus. This brain structure plays a central role in memory, learning, and spatial navigation. For instance, remembering the name of someone you just met or finding your way through an unfamiliar place depends on the hippocampus. It also connects emotions to memories, which is why emotionally intense experiences tend to stay with us longer. Importantly, the hippocampus is one of the few areas in the adult brain that continues to produce new neurons. This process is vital for maintaining memory, enhancing learning ability, and building resilience to stress.

Scientific research backs up the benefits of exercise on the hippocampus. A 2006 study from the University of Illinois found that regular aerobic exercise helped adults maintain the volume of their hippocampus, slowing memory decline associated with aging. Another study revealed that older adults who walked three times a week for a year experienced a 1–2 percent increase in hippocampal volume, along with noticeable memory improvements.

Exercise also activates the frontal lobe, another critical brain region. The frontal lobe is responsible for regulating emotions, thoughts, and higher-level cognitive functions like setting goals, planning, and staying focused. A 2015 study conducted by researchers at New York University explored the impact of a single session of aerobic exercise on brain function. The study found that participants showed improved performance on tasks requiring decision-making, attention, and self-control. The findings show that even brief sessions of aerobic exercise can boost cognitive functions linked to the frontal lobe, underscoring its significant benefits for brain health.

Another way exercise benefits the brain is by improving neuroplasticity—the brain's ability to adapt by forming and strengthening connections between nerve cells. This adaptability is supported by a protein called brain-derived neurotrophic factor (BDNF). Often likened to a "fertilizer for the brain," BDNF promotes the growth and survival of nerve cells, helping them connect more effectively, which in turn strengthens memory and learning. Research has shown that engaging in high-intensity aerobic exercise can significantly increase BDNF levels, making it easier for the brain to process and retain new information.

Exercise doesn't just offer short-term benefits like improved mood and focus—it also has long-term effects on brain health. Regular physical activity has been shown to reduce the risk of neurodegenerative diseases. A 2017 study from the University of British Columbia found that regular physical activity lowers the risk of developing Alzheimer's disease. It also showed that exercise improves daily functioning and mobility in people already living with the condition.

Incorporating regular exercise into your life is a powerful way to boost brain function, maintain cognitive health, and safeguard against memory decline. Whether it's a brisk walk, run, or strength training, the benefits for your brain are undeniable.

Exercise Boosts Creativity

There is extensive research showing that exercise improves creativity. For example, a 2014 Stanford University study found that walking significantly boosts creative thinking. Participants generated far more creative ideas while walking compared to sitting, with creativity increasing by about 60 percent during walking sessions.

A 2021 study conducted by researchers at the University of Graz, Austria, further explored the connection between physical activity and creativity. Participants wore activity trackers for five days to measure their daily exercise levels and then completed a creativity test. The results showed that those who were more physically active had more creative thoughts. Researchers explained this link by noting that physical activity helps reduce stress, promotes neuroplasticity, and broadens the range and flexibility of thinking.

Throughout history, many influential figures have recognized the mental benefits of exercise and incorporated it into their lives. While we often imagine great philosophers, scientists, and artists hunched over desks or buried in books, many of them valued physical fitness and made exercise a key part of their routines.

Socrates, for example, believed that physical fitness was essential for mental and moral growth and was known for his physical strength and endurance. His student Plato, who was also a wrestler, earned his name from his "broad shoulders." Marie Curie, the pioneering chemist, was an avid cyclist and spent her honeymoon cycling through the French countryside. Author Haruki Murakami credits running 10 kilometers daily with giving him the physical and mental stamina needed to write novels.

Walking has long been used as a tool for reflection, creativity, and inspiration. German philosopher Friedrich Nietzsche famously said, "All truly great thoughts are conceived while walking." He spent hours each day walking in nature, using this time to develop his ideas. Many of his writings were inspired during these long walks. Nietzsche believed that modern life weakens people and argued that activities like walking are essential to building mental strength and resilience.

Henry David Thoreau saw walking in nature as essential to his creative life. He described it as a way to connect with wildness and free himself from worldly engagements. "The moment my legs begin to move," he wrote, "my thoughts begin to flow." Thoreau often spent several hours a day sauntering through fields and forests, treating it as a spiritual practice.

Humans evolved through movement. Our ancestors survived by walking, running, hunting, and engaging their bodies daily. These physical activities were directly linked to the development of the brain, enabling skills like tool-making, strategic thinking, and adaptation to changing environments. Movement wasn't just about survival—it was key to human progress.

In today's world, reduced movement takes a clear toll: both the body and brain grow weaker. Physical and mental functions decline, and we lose energy and vitality. Exercise is not just a means to maintain health—it's a fundamental activity that keeps our brain and body working as they should. Movement is natural for humans, and exercise remains one of the most effective ways to unlock the full potential of our body and brain, improving both their performance and value.

Exercise Cultivates Self-Understanding

Exercise is a practical and effective way to deepen self-understanding. It enhances interoception, our ability to sense what is happening inside our bodies with greater clarity and awareness. This includes recognizing physical states like hunger, thirst, and fatigue, as well as emotional responses like tension, relaxation, and anxiety. Developing interoceptive awareness allows us to better understand and respond to the signals from our body and mind, especially during moments of stress or tension. This awareness is the foundation of self-care and self-knowledge.

Exercise strengthens interoceptive awareness because it naturally brings attention to physical sensations. When we exercise, we notice our heart beating, the rhythm of our breathing, and how our muscles tense and relax. Paying attention to these signals builds a stronger connection with our bodies.

For example, when you run, you can feel your heart beating faster, its rhythm echoing through your body, your breathing becoming deeper and more regular, and the steady impact of your feet hitting the ground. These sensations create a powerful awareness of your body and a vivid sense of vitality—a feeling of being truly alive.

Focusing on your body's movements during exercise can also lead to a state of immersion, similar to meditation. Psychologist Mihaly Csikszentmihalyi called this the "flow" state—when you are so absorbed in an activity that time seems to fade, and the boundary between yourself and your surroundings blurs. In this state, your senses become sharper, your thoughts quiet down, and you are fully present in the moment.

This immersive effect is particularly noticeable in aerobic exercises like walking or running, where the repetitive, rhythmic movements calm the mind and bring a sense of stability and peace. Similarly, slower, mindful exercises such as qigong or yoga help quiet mental chatter and allow you to experience a deep state of focus and inner stillness. In this state, sometimes described as "no-self," you feel a complete sense of oneness with your surroundings. The usual sense of separation fades away, leaving you fully present, connected, and in harmony with the moment.

Interestingly, the effects of exercise often complement those of meditation. While exercise primarily begins with the body, its benefits naturally extend to the mind, preparing it for greater clarity and focus. Similarly, meditation works inwardly to refine and sharpen the mind, enhancing its connection to the body. Together, these practices highlight the deep connection between the mind and body, each supporting the other in fostering overall well-being.

By paying attention to your body through exercise, you naturally learn more about your mind. This connection helps you manage stress, build awareness, and cultivate a sense of balance. If you're looking for a simple yet powerful way to create meaningful change in your life, starting with exercise is one of the best steps you can take.

Three Physical Brain Sports Practices

I recommend walking, strength training, and gut exercises as practical Brain Sports that anyone can incorporate into their daily routine. Each exercise provides an opportunity to awaken your BrainPhone, strengthen neural pathways, and develop mental focus alongside physical strength.

When engaging in Brain Sports, don't just move your body—stay mindful of your brain. Being mindful of your brain doesn't mean thinking about it directly; it means tuning into each movement, noticing how your body feels, and staying fully present in the moment. See each exercise as a chance to train your brain and tap into your potential, rather than simply going through the motions. Notice how each movement impacts your body and mind, and enjoy the process. This mindset turns exercise into a valuable way to build your strength, focus, and overall well-being.

LONGEVITY WALKING

Walking is one of the simplest yet most effective forms of exercise, offering widely recognized benefits. It strengthens the heart, boosts brain function, supports bone and joint health, releases feel-good hormones, reduces depression, and improves sleep. When approached mindfully, walking becomes more than just a way to get from one place to another—it becomes a form of meditation, a time to recharge, restore balance, and heal both the body and mind.

To practice Longevity Walking, begin by standing comfortably with your shoulders relaxed and your chest open. Keep your lower back straight yet relaxed. Then, tilt your entire body slightly forward, about 1–2 degrees. You're not bending at the waist or leaning your upper body forward; you're shifting your entire posture slightly ahead. This small adjustment naturally makes your brain feel more alert and focused while improving your overall balance.

If you observe children, they walk with their bodies leaning forward, light on their feet, as if ready to spring into action. As we age, we tend to lean back slightly and develop a heavier, unsteady gait. Longevity Walking helps reverse this old gait and restore a more natural, youthful way of walking that feels lighter and more energetic.

To bring more awareness to your walk, focus on the balls of your feet. As you stand, flex your toes slightly, feeling them grip the ground. While walking, step lightly with your heel, press firmly with the ball of your foot, and push off with your big toe. Imagine the balls of your feet pressing buttons on the ground with each step. Since the soles of your feet are connected to the rest of your body through nerve endings, evenly stimulating them as you walk can feel like a full-body massage.

Keep your feet aligned side by side, pointing forward in a figure 11. Allow your arms to swing naturally and walk with a relaxed smile on your face. Focus on making your movements light, balanced, and smooth—not heavy or stumbling. Relax your body as you walk, keeping your center of gravity steady on the balls of your feet as you press each into the ground. With each step, feel your weight shifting evenly and naturally from one foot to the other, creating a calm and regular rhythm. This mindful approach allows you to experience a smoother flow of energy throughout your body, making your walk both revitalizing and balanced.

Once you become comfortable with Longevity Walking, try taking longer strides or walking at a faster pace. Longer strides engage more leg muscles and improve blood circulation, while walking faster also increases heart rate. These adjustments boost the benefits of aerobic exercise—such as enhancing oxygen flow to the brain—which helps sharpen brain function. Faster walking and longer strides also help restore energy and are especially effective in strengthening overall cardiovascular function, which naturally weakens with age. These simple enhancements can turn walking into a powerful way to improve overall health.

STRENGTH TRAINING

Strength training isn't just about building muscle—it's a powerful tool for maintaining overall health and well-being. As we age, muscle loss naturally occurs, but strength training helps prevent this decline. Strengthening muscles improves posture, reduces the risk of injury, and enhances overall physical performance. It also boosts your metabolism, making it easier to manage your weight. Beyond building muscle, strength training benefits your bones, supports heart health, and helps regulate blood sugar levels.

The mental benefits of strength training are just as significant. Like other forms of exercise, it reduces stress, calms the nervous system, and alleviates anxiety and worry. It's also been shown to improve focus, enhance sleep quality, support learning, and slow brain aging, helping to keep your mind sharp and resilient.

To get started with strength training, focus on bodyweight exercises such as push-ups, sit-ups, lunges, and squats. These foundational movements are simple, effective, and require no equipment. As your strength improves, you can gradually incorporate machines, dumbbells, or weights to target specific muscle groups and increase resistance.

Aim for three sets of 10 to 15 repetitions of each exercise, using an intensity appropriate for your fitness level. Avoid lifting weights that are too heavy too soon, as this can lead to injury. Instead, progress gradually by increasing weight, repetitions, or duration as your body adapts and grows stronger.

If you're short on time, "one-minute workouts" are a practical solution. Quick exercises like push-ups, squats, sit-ups, or planks can be done for just one minute at a time, making it easier to stay active throughout the day. Setting a timer or reminder every hour can encourage consistency. Ten short bursts of exercise spread across the day can add up, delivering noticeable benefits for your body and mind.

Remember, a one-minute workout can easily be extended if you have more time. Stretch it to five or ten minutes or combine multiple exercises into a quick, effective set. For example, start with push-ups or sit-ups, add a minute of plank, and finish with squats or lunges. These short sessions will quickly elevate your heart rate, boost blood flow, activate your muscles, and leave you feeling recharged and energized.

If you're new to strength training, don't be surprised if you feel some muscle soreness at first. It's a sign that your body is adapting. To support recovery, mix in light activities like stretching or gentle movement. Over time, these small efforts will build strength, improve your health, and leave you feeling more capable and resilient every day.

INTESTINE EXERCISE

Your gut, often called your "second brain," plays a critical role in your overall health and well-being. With more nerve cells than the brain, the gut does much more than digest food. It influences your emotions, mental health, breathing, blood pressure, flexibility, and energy levels. About 70 percent of your immune system is located in your gut, and 95 percent of your serotonin—the happy hormone—is produced there.

While eating well, staying hydrated, managing stress, and exercising regularly are important for gut health, many people also rely on fermented foods like kimchi or probiotic supplements. However, a simple and practical way to improve gut health and boost energy is through Intestine Exercise, which directly activates and strengthens the gut.

To practice Intestine Exercise, focus on your lower abdomen and repeatedly pull in and release your belly. As you pull in, tighten your abdomen as deeply as possible, as if trying to draw it toward your spine. Gently contract your anus to enhance the effect. When releasing, let your abdomen expand slowly and naturally, feeling the gentle pressure build, as though you're inflating a balloon.

Start with about 50 repetitions and gradually increase as your strength improves. As you get more comfortable, aim for 300 reps or more. With regular practice, you can build up to 1,000 reps in about 10 minutes, at a pace of around 100 reps per minute. Doing this daily creates a warm, energizing sensation in your lower abdomen, promoting the ideal energy balance of a "cool head and a warm belly." This energy state leaves you feeling focused, grounded, and revitalized.

The benefits of Intestine Exercise aren't limited to digestion. Practicing it improves blood flow and energy circulation, helping you feel refreshed and more alive. It also supports deeper, steadier breathing, which calms your mind, lowers stress, and improves focus. If you're often tired or worn out, this simple exercise can help restore your energy, improve your stamina, and speed up your recovery.

Intestine Exercise is easy to fit into your day. It's an energizing way to wake up in the morning, and it can help you fight fatigue and recharge in the evening. By strengthening your gut, you're giving your body and mind a simple, effective tool to feel stronger, clearer, and more balanced every day.

CHAPTER 9

MEDITATE TO STAY AWAKE

Meditation is more than just a way to relax. It's the most essential and powerful Brain Sport, forming the foundation for unlocking your brain's full potential. By connecting your brain, body, and spirit, meditation helps you cut through distractions, sharpen focus, and expand awareness, giving you the tools to take control of your mind.

While physical exercises like pull-ups build physical strength and mental resilience, meditation works from the inside out, restoring balance and awakening creativity. In this chapter, you'll explore how meditation, as the cornerstone of Brain Sports, helps you reset your brain, ignite your inner potential, and keep your BrainPhone fully activated, empowering you to live fully awake in every moment.

The Zero Point Reset

Every day, a constant stream of external stimuli surrounds us. With so much information and so many distractions competing for our attention, our minds can easily become scattered, losing touch with what's happening within us. Meditation is a way to shift this outward focus inward, helping us reconnect with ourselves and restore our natural sense of harmony and peace. By turning inward, we can reset our minds, cultivate clarity, and regain balance amidst the chaos of daily life.

Meditation does this by helping re-center the brain's "zero point," restoring its natural balance. Imagine the brain as a scale: if you place heavy objects on the scale repeatedly, its balance shifts, and it can no longer measure accurately. Similarly, our mind can become unbalanced from the ongoing weight of thoughts, emotions, and habits. Meditation acts like a reset, helping the brain regain its natural equilibrium and harmony.

An essential part of this process is developing "observer consciousness." This feature is like the mind's eye—a clear, impartial awareness that sees your thoughts and emotions as they are without trying to judge or label them. Without this awareness, your emotional reactions of the moment become a preoccupation. Fixating on the particular emotions of the situation, you become trapped in a spiral of more thoughts, which in turn becomes overwhelming. When this happens, you lose perspective and become consumed by your thoughts and emotions, unable to see them as separate from yourself.

The key to observer consciousness is creating space between yourself and your thoughts or emotions. When thoughts and emotions feel too close, viewing them objectively is difficult. It's like holding a mirror too close to your face—you can't see the full picture. Stepping back allows you to observe your thoughts and emotions from a distance, creating the space needed to reflect on, regulate, and even transform them. At this point, your thoughts and emotions become tools you can work with, rather than forces that control you.

Thoughts and emotions are like weather. They come and go, influenced by external circumstances. Just as we can't stop it from raining or getting cold, we can't prevent thoughts and emotions from arising. But we can adapt to them, like using an umbrella in the rain or bundling up in the cold. Observer consciousness allows us to see these mental and emotional events as transient, ever-changing phenomena. This perspective helps us stay calm and centered without becoming overly attached to them.

Meditation isn't about getting rid of thoughts or emotions; it's about observing them without reaction. A calm, non-judgmental observer has the power to bring everything back into harmony. When we observe thoughts without reacting, they stop spiraling. When we observe emotions without resistance, they gradually lose their intensity, freeing us from being swept away by them.

Observer awareness also shines a light on the patterns of thought and behavior we unconsciously repeat. It helps us notice how we react to situations, what triggers certain thoughts and emotions, and the habits that shape our responses. This awareness allows us to grow beyond automatic reactions and make more conscious and intentional choices. It also helps release old emotional residues and memories, leading to clearer thinking and healthier, more positive habits.

Meditation Brings Emotional Balance

Meditation is essential if you want to live a more aware and intentional life. It creates real, noticeable changes in your brain and body, helping you build a more balanced emotional foundation. And there's solid research to back this up.

Physically, meditation changes your brain. A 2009 UCLA study found that long-term meditators have a larger hippocampus, a brain region involved in memory, and a bigger orbitofrontal cortex, which is critical for emotional control. These changes help you stay calm and collected, even in difficult situations.

Meditation also calms your amygdala, the brain's alarm system that activates during fear or stress. While the amygdala is essential for handling danger, the constant stress of modern life can keep it overactive, leading to chronic anxiety. In a study led by Gaëlle Desbordes, participants in an eight-week meditation program showed less amygdala activity, even when they weren't meditating. This means the benefits of meditation extend far beyond practice sessions.

On a chemical level, meditation boosts feel-good hormones like serotonin and endorphins. It also helps your body manage stress more effectively by activating the parasympathetic nervous system. This system counteracts the effects of the stress-driven "fight-or-flight" response, promoting a state of relaxation and recovery. It slows your heart rate, reduces stress hormones, and promotes deep relaxation, providing a solid foundation for emotional balance.

Meditation helps you step back and observe your thoughts and emotions without getting caught up in them, awakening your observer consciousness. This shift makes it easier to break out of cycles of worry or overthinking and process emotions in healthier ways.

It also nurtures kindness and compassion, both toward others and yourself. This strengthens relationships, boosts emotional resilience, and builds self-confidence. When you approach challenges with self-compassion and understanding, they often feel far more manageable.

All these benefits add up to make meditation a life-changing tool for emotional well-being. Whether you're seeking balance, deeper connections, or a greater sense of peace, meditation can help you get there.

Meditation Enhances Cognitive Performance

Studies show that meditation fosters attention, memory, and creativity, making it go-to practice for improving mental performance. Even a short period of practice can deliver impressive results. In a 2007 study, Dr. Yi-Yuan Tang found that just five days of meditation combining relaxation, mental imagery, and mindfulness improved attention and self-regulation. It also activated brain regions responsible for emotional control and cognitive focus, proving that even a brief commitment to meditation can sharpen focus and mental clarity.

Long-term meditation takes these benefits to the next level. Research led by Dr. Sara Lazar in 2005 revealed that experienced meditators have thicker cortical regions in areas like the prefrontal cortex and right anterior insula, which are critical for attention and sensory processing. Regular meditation strengthens cognitive control and enhances the brain's structural health over time.

The benefits aren't just structural. Meditation trains you to stay present, manage distractions, and approach problems with clarity. It improves blood flow to the brain, delivering oxygen and nutrients essential for memory and decision-making. A study from the Max Planck Institute for Human Cognitive and Brain Sciences found that six months of meditation practice reduced cortisol levels—a major stress hormone—by 25 percent, improving concentration and clear thinking.

One study led by Fadel Zeidan found that meditation significantly improves metacognitive awareness and working memory. Metacognition is the ability to observe and manage your own thoughts and plays a critical role in decision-making and self-control. Participants in the study reported better focus and greater control over their mental processes, showing how consistent meditation practice can enhance cognitive function and mental performance.

By combining structural, physiological, and psychological benefits, meditation provides a grounded base for enduring mental sharpness and resilience.

Meditation Sustains Your Brain for a Lifetime

Meditation is a powerful tool for protecting and enhancing brain health as we age. Research shows that regular meditation can slow cognitive decline, preserve mental sharpness, and promote vitality, making it valuable at any stage of life.

A 2014 UCLA study revealed that long-term meditators experience significantly less gray matter loss with age compared to non-meditators. Since gray matter is essential for processing information and making decisions, meditation's role in preserving its density helps keep the brain sharper for longer.

Meditation benefits extend beyond the brain to the cellular level. A Harvard study led by Dr. Elizabeth Hoge found that experienced meditators have longer telomeres. Telomeres are the protective caps on chromosomes that play a critical role in cellular health and longevity. Female meditators showed particularly significant results, suggesting meditation may slow biological aging and enhance cellular resilience.

Meditation also fosters neuroplasticity—the brain's natural ability to adapt and reorganize itself. By reinforcing neural connections, it safeguards essential functions like memory and emotional regulation, promoting steady mental agility and balance over time.

Stress, a major contributor to aging and disease, is another area where meditation shines. By lowering cortisol levels and calming the nervous system, it reduces the damaging effects of chronic stress. It also fosters positive emotions like gratitude and compassion, linked to better cardiovascular health, a stronger immune system, and greater emotional resilience.

Other benefits include improved sleep quality, essential for cellular repair and cognitive longevity, and increased production of mood-regulating neurotransmitters. Meditation also enhances self-awareness and emotional stability, promoting healthier lifestyle choices that support overall vitality and well-being. Whether you start early or later in life, the practice lays a strong foundation for a healthier, longer, and more vibrant life.

Meditation Gives Your Brain a True Rest

Your brain has a "default mode network" (DMN) that becomes active when you're not focused on a specific task. This network engages during rest or relaxation, allowing your brain to reflect on past experiences, plan for the future, and think about yourself. The DMN plays a key role in introspection, emotional regulation, and self-awareness. It's also where creative thinking, problem-solving, and imagining new possibilities happen, as it connects past experiences to potential outcomes.

While the DMN is essential for reflection and creativity, too much activity in this network can have negative effects. Research links an overactive DMN to mental health challenges like depression and anxiety, as well as conditions like Alzheimer's, ADHD, and PTSD. You've likely experienced this when your mind spirals into worry, replaying past mistakes, dwelling on resentment, or feeling stuck in self-doubt. Even when your body is at rest, this mental overdrive can be exhausting.

Meditation offers a way to break this cycle by calming the overactive DMN and restoring balance. Research by Dr. Judson Brewer at Yale University shows that experienced meditators have significantly less DMN activity during meditation. Through observer consciousness—stepping back and watching your thoughts without reacting—meditation helps shift unproductive mental loops into constructive, creative, and positive thinking.

Meditation also teaches your brain to transition seamlessly between intense focus and relaxed, free-flowing thoughts. Typically, focusing on a task requires blocking out unrelated thoughts, while relaxation allows your mind to wander freely. Meditation blends these states by creating a state of relaxed concentration. In this state, you maintain focus without tension while staying open to fresh ideas and insights. For instance, during meditation, you might focus on your breath while observing your thoughts without judgment. This calm yet alert state fosters an ideal environment for creativity and innovation, often sparking fresh ideas and solutions.

By embracing meditation, you give your brain the gift of balance—calming the overactive loops of the default mode network while fostering the relaxed concentration needed for creativity and clarity. In doing so, you provide your brain with true rest, allowing it to recharge and function at its best. This practice helps you step out of unproductive thought spirals and into a space where reflection and innovation coexist.

Meditation Cultivates Acceptance

One powerful benefit of meditation is its ability to cultivate acceptance. True acceptance doesn't mean ignoring injustice or surrendering to defeat; it means recognizing and acknowledging situations, people, and yourself as they are. This mindset allows you to engage with reality more effectively without resistance, denial, or criticism.

Meditation expands your awareness and perspective, naturally increasing your capacity for acceptance. When focused only on your needs or desires, accepting outcomes that don't align with what you want can be challenging. But meditation helps you see the bigger picture, including other viewpoints and the full context of situations. With this expanded perspective, you're better equipped to respond to challenges with clarity and effective action.

Struggling with acceptance often leads to emotional and mental turmoil. Suppressing or denying feelings like sadness or anger can make them more intense, turning them into persistent sources of anxiety or stress. Without acceptance, your perspective can become clouded, making it harder to see situations clearly or address the root causes of problems. This lack of acceptance can also lead to blame—toward yourself or others—creating unnecessary tension and conflict in relationships.

Meditation is a powerful way to build acceptance because it strengthens self-awareness and emotional regulation. When you meditate, you practice observing your thoughts and emotions as they arise, without suppressing or judging them. This builds the habit of accepting challenging emotions and situations in your daily life. Meditation also calms the amygdala and activates the prefrontal cortex, the brain region responsible for emotional regulation. This process lowers anxiety and stress, making it easier for you to handle emotions with grace and flexibility.

Acceptance nurtures resilience. It helps you recover from setbacks and adapt to challenges with confidence. When you learn to accept pain or disappointment, you reduce your fear of change and gain the flexibility to navigate life's difficulties. This mindset gives you the strength to face obstacles with a clear head and steady heart.

Meditation teaches you to approach uncomfortable experiences, relationships, and emotions as they are, rather than avoiding or resisting them. This shift empowers you to take proactive steps toward solving problems, rather than feeling stuck or helpless.

Mindset for Meditation

People come to meditation for many practical reasons, such as reducing stress, improving sleep, or enhancing focus, and for spiritual motivations, such as seeking meaning or awakening. Meditation can support all of these goals, and many people notice positive changes in their bodies and minds, bringing them closer to the life they want.

However, the most effective mindset for meditation is one of no purpose. While meditation can serve many purposes, its deepest intention is to restore a free and calm state of mind without reliance on specific outcomes or external conditions. This idea aligns with the concepts of "resetting the brain to zero-point" and "observer consciousness" discussed earlier.

However, you don't need to abandon the reason you started meditating. If you're meditating to reduce stress, improve focus, or achieve another specific goal, that's perfectly fine. Start with whatever purpose feels meaningful to you. Over time, as you practice, you may find meditation enjoyable for its own sake. With continued practice, you'll experience the more profound nature of meditation beyond the initial goals that brought you to it.

Regardless of your starting point, meditation naturally leads to self-exploration. At our core, we all desire to understand ourselves better, though we often lose touch with this longing amid busy schedules and constant external demands. Meditation reawakens this inner desire and guides us toward authentic self-discovery. It is not simply a tool to achieve a specific outcome; it is a journey into yourself and the essence of life.

The right mindset for meditation involves honesty, humility, and open-mindedness. Honesty allows you to face your thoughts, emotions, and limitations as they are. Since meditation is about self-reflection, avoiding or deceiving yourself can block meaningful growth.

Humility is essential in meditation because it allows you to approach the practice with a willingness to learn and grow, acknowledging that you don't have all the answers. It helps you let go of the need to control or judge your experiences, creating space for genuine insight and transformation. Humility reminds you that meditation is not about achieving perfection or mastery but about being open to what arises, no matter how small or subtle the lessons may seem.

Open-mindedness complements this by encouraging you to accept each experience as it unfolds without trying to fit it into preconceived ideas or expectations. Together, these qualities form the foundation for a deeper, more meaningful meditation practice.

Meditation can offer many wonderful benefits when approached with honesty, humility, and open-mindedness. It can improve physical and mental health, clarify long-standing questions, and foster inner peace and self-awareness. However, these are not the ultimate goals of meditation; they are natural outcomes of engaging openly and honestly with yourself.

Approach meditation with curiosity and a genuine desire to know yourself. Accept each experience as it comes, with gratitude and openness. As you continue, meditation will free your mind from limitations and allow you to see life with greater clarity and fresh perspective.

Recommended Meditation Practices

Any meditation that helps reset your brain to its zero point while awakening your observer consciousness can be beneficial. Among these, I recommend three types of meditation: energy-sensing meditation, breathing meditation, and dynamic meditation, which involves movement.

These meditations are particularly effective because they focus on energy sensations, breathing, and movement, making it easier for beginners to connect with their observer consciousness. Concentrating on specific sensations makes them straightforward and accessible, even for those new to meditation. You can find detailed instructions for energy sensing on page 80 and for breathing meditations on page 94.

Dynamic meditations, such as Shaking Meditation and Brain Wave Vibration, are excellent starting points. These practices engage the body and help prepare the mind for deeper relaxation and focus. After practicing a dynamic meditation, you can transition to energy sensing or breathing meditation to deepen your experience and gain even greater benefit.

SHAKING MEDITATION

When we think of meditation, we often picture sitting still with our eyes closed. However, meditation can also be practiced through movement. Dynamic meditations such as Shaking Meditation can be as effective as traditional seated meditation. Shaking Meditation involves gently and rhythmically moving your body to create light vibrations, allowing you to enter a meditative state in a very short time. These vibrations are highly effective at quieting the mind's chatter and bringing awareness to the body.

Think of how we naturally use repetitive motions to comfort and relax. For instance, when soothing babies, we rock the cradle, pace with them in our arms, or gently pat their backs. These motions create a sense of safety and calm. Similarly, when you're anxious or nervous, you might instinctively shake your legs or pace, which is your body's natural way of releasing tension through movement and vibration.

To begin Shaking Meditation, stand comfortably with your feet shoulder-width apart and your knees slightly bent. Relax your neck and shoulders, straighten your back, and let your arms hang naturally at your sides. Take a few deep breaths, then begin to gently bounce or recoil into your legs, creating a rhythmic shaking motion. Allow your entire body to participate—feel your spine move, your chest and shoulders relax, and your arms sway freely. Let the vibrations travel through your jaw and neck, loosening any tightness and spreading the relaxation to your entire face. Feel your cheeks soften, your forehead smooth out, and your eyes relax as the gentle vibrations ease away any tension.

Focus on the balls of your feet and feel your weight sink naturally into the soles of your feet. Move at a pace and intensity that feels comfortable for you. As you continue, you may naturally exhale with a "hoo" sound, releasing tension and stress with each breath. After shaking for 3–5 minutes, you'll notice your body warming up and your breathing deepening. Your joints and muscles will feel looser, and your mind will be calmer. When you stop shaking, stand comfortably and breathe naturally for another minute or so, focusing on the subtle vibrations that linger in your body.

Shaking Meditation is an easy-to-follow yet effective practice for releasing physical and mental tension, calming the mind, and reconnecting with your body. It's an accessible way to experience meditation through movement, bringing relaxation and awareness into your daily life.

BRAIN WAVE VIBRATION

Brain Wave Vibration is a dynamic meditation practice that uses gentle movement and rhythmic tapping to stabilize brainwaves and promote relaxation. It involves gently rocking your neck from side to side while rhythmically tapping your lower abdomen with your fists. This technique effectively calms the mind, relieves tension, and supports overall well-being.

A 2012 study by the University of London and the Korea Institute of Brain Science found that Brain Wave Vibration can improve mood, boost energy levels, reduce stress, and increase self-awareness. The study also noted that this practice can be more effective than static meditation for relieving depression and helping people fall asleep more quickly.

When stressed, tension often builds at the first cervical vertebra, where the skull meets the neck. If left unresolved, this tension can cause neck, shoulders, and upper spine stiffness, leading to discomfort throughout the upper body. Brain Wave Vibration helps release this tension naturally through gentle neck movements and rhythmic tapping, which relax the body and improve circulation.

To practice Brain Wave Vibration, start by standing or sitting comfortably. Gently rock your neck from side to side in a soothing motion. At the same time, form light fists with both hands and rhythmically tap your lower abdomen, alternating hands and using the pinky side of your fists. Breathe out slowly through your mouth as you continue tapping. As you rock your head, focus on the steady center axis within your body. This axis, where the spine aligns and the autonomic nerves are located, is essential for maintaining balance and stability.

Start with slow, gentle neck movements, gradually increasing the speed and intensity as you feel more comfortable. If you notice heavy or warm sensations in your head, exhale deeply through your mouth to release them. This process helps ease tension in your neck and improves blood flow and energy circulation to your head, making it feel cooler and lighter. Meanwhile, the rhythmic tapping on your lower abdomen generates warmth, creating a sense of balance. This state, known as Water Up, Fire Down, reflects an optimal energy balance where your head feels cool and your abdomen warm, supporting both physical relaxation and mental clarity. From this balanced state, you can naturally enter a state of relaxed concentration.

The practice of Brain Wave Vibration can last anywhere from 3 minutes to 20 minutes or longer, depending on your needs. After completing the practice, place your hands in your lap and take a few moments to breathe naturally. Allow yourself to feel the sensations in your body as your breathing stabilizes and deepens. Many people notice a sense of calm, gratitude, and inner peace during this phase of the practice.

This practical and effective meditation technique helps release physical tension and mental stress and enhances your awareness and connection to your body. It's an effective way to restore balance and clarity, leaving you feeling refreshed and grounded in both mind and body.

Qigong, A Moving Meditation

In addition to meditation, one practice I highly recommend for its profound and wide-ranging benefits is qigong. As a key element of Brain Sports, qigong stands out because it incorporates physical movement and energy flow into the practice. At its core, qigong is about sensing energy and directing its flow through focused awareness, which is why it is often referred to as a moving meditation.

Qigong offers both the mental clarity and relaxation of traditional meditation and the added benefits of gentle movements. By simultaneously focusing on body movement, energy flow, and breathing, qigong helps your brain become more aware of and in control of your body's sensations.

What makes qigong such a powerful Brain Sport is its ability to teach you how to use your mind with intention. Qigong is based on the principle, "Where the mind goes, energy flows." This phrase means that wherever you focus your attention, energy is directed and activated in that area.

For example, when you first train your energy senses, you might focus your awareness on your hands. With practice, you may feel sensations such as warmth, tingling, or a fuzzy energy vibration in your hands. Similarly, if you focus on your lower abdomen while breathing and imagine energy gathering there, you may notice a warm, full sensation in that area.

These experiences show that you can control the intensity and direction of energy using your mind, enabling you to change the state of your body and brain. Through qigong, you realize that the energy you feel and move is not separate from your mind but your mind in action.

As you become more skilled at using your mind in this way, you'll learn to direct energy beyond your body. You can send energy to objects, places, or goals, regardless of time or distance. For example, you can send comfort and healing energy to someone far away, channel your energy toward achieving a specific goal, or even send blessings and healing to the earth and all living beings.

Qigong teaches you not only how to sense and direct energy but also how to connect with the world through it. By working with energy through focused awareness, qigong deepens your ability to feel and strengthens your connection to humanity, nature, and the universe. It invites you to move beyond individual concerns and engage with the larger web of life.

If you're curious about this transformative practice, here are two simple qigong exercises perfect for beginners. These practices will help you start sensing energy and experiencing the unique harmony of mind, body, and breath that qigong offers.

ENERGY RECHARGE WALK

Energy Recharge Walk is a mindful practice that combines your steps, breathing, and awareness of energy flow through your body. To begin, stand comfortably with your feet shoulder-width apart and your arms hanging naturally at your sides. Rotate your wrists so that your palms face forward. This simple adjustment helps open your chest and lower back, stabilizing your posture and allowing energy to flow more smoothly through your body.

Hold this position and start walking rhythmically at a steady, smooth pace—almost like a cat's graceful, deliberate steps. Be mindful of how the soles of your feet connect with the ground with each step, and pay attention to the energy flowing through your body. With every step, feel energy rising through the soles of your feet and circulating into your palms, creating a continuous flow throughout your body.

The key is to keep your pace natural while staying fully aware of the sensation of energy moving through your feet, palms, and body. To deepen the experience, synchronize your walking with your breathing. For example, take three steps while inhaling through your nose, then three steps while exhaling through your mouth. As you become comfortable with this rhythm, gradually extend your breathing to four or five steps per inhale and exhale, depending on what feels natural.

QIGONG SQUATS

Qigong Squats are a powerful practice that transcends the simple act of sitting down and standing up. By combining mindful movement, intentional breathing, and energy awareness, they harmonize the body and mind, offering a dynamic exercise that builds physical strength while fostering inner balance and mental clarity.

To begin, stand comfortably with your feet shoulder-width apart, keeping your back straight and your arms relaxed by your sides. Breathe naturally, allowing your mind to become calm and focused. As you inhale through your nose, gently push your hips back and bend your knees, lowering yourself into a squat position. As you go down, extend your arms outward in a half-circle, palms facing up. Imagine a warm, soft energy gathering in your palms as you hold this position.

As you exhale through your mouth, slowly rise back to a standing position while bringing your hands together at the center of your body. Turn your palms downward and imagine gently pushing the gathered energy down into the ground. Visualize a powerful surge of energy radiating from your body's center, traveling down through your legs, and deeply rooting into the earth. Feel the upward momentum as if your body is being propelled by the energy, much like a rocket launching upward.

Repeat this sequence 10 times, staying mindful of the energy moving through your legs and pelvis. With each repetition, feel the strengthening and activation of your bones, joints, tendons, ligaments, and muscles. Focus on the sensation of energy circulating throughout your body with each movement.

Though this movement may seem like a simple squat variation on the surface, it is, in fact, a profound qigong practice that weaves together imagination, energy awareness, and physical movement. This integration enhances your body's natural healing capacity and awakens your creative potential. Through Qigong Squats, you build physical strength while deepening your connection to your body and mind, unlocking a sense of balance, vitality, and inner harmony that transcends physical exercise.

CHAPTER 10

BE POSITIVE AND GRATEFUL

Gratitude and positivity are the mindsets that supercharge the effectiveness of Brain Sports and activate your BrainPhone to its fullest potential. They create a foundation for resilience, helping you navigate challenges with clarity and turn setbacks into opportunities for growth. By focusing on what's good and expressing appreciation, you unlock a natural flow of energy that fuels creativity, clarity, and well-being.

Yet, cultivating this mindset requires effort because our brains are naturally wired to prioritize negativity. Have you ever received 10 compliments from your boss, yet one piece of negative feedback overshadows all the praise? The "good job" comments fade quickly, while the critical remark lingers, stirring self-doubt and anxiety. This isn't a reflection of your capabilities. It's simply your brain's natural tendency, called "negativity bias," to focus on negative information and hold on to it longer to guard against potential threats.

This bias, which developed in early human history as a survival mechanism, still shapes our responses today. While it once helped our ancestors remain vigilant to dangers, in modern life, it often magnifies minor setbacks and diminishes positive experiences, making it harder to maintain balance and perspective.

A single negative comment on social media can ruin an otherwise great day, replaying in your mind and stealing your joy. News stories follow the same pattern—scandals and disasters dominate headlines, leaving acts of kindness or progress in the shadows.

Negative emotions aren't inherently bad; they serve valuable purposes in our lives. Fear keeps us alert to danger, while sadness helps us process loss and facilitates healing. The problem arises when negativity bias dominates our thinking, draining joy and hope. This can leave us feeling stuck, unable to pursue our goals or see possibilities beyond our doubts.

The good news is that you can retrain your brain. Thanks to neuroplasticity, your brain adapts to what you focus on and experience repeatedly. By intentionally practicing positivity and gratitude, you can loosen the grip of negativity bias and rewire your mind to view life with greater balance and clarity. As you make this shift, you'll start to see things more clearly, appreciate the good in your life, and build the resilience to move forward with hope and confidence.

The Power of Absolute Positivity

Our brains cannot tell the difference between imagination and reality, so even negative thoughts, without any actual negative events, can trigger stress hormones, putting strain on the body and mind. When negative thinking is repeated, the brain responds automatically with a negative outlook, defaulting to seeing situations through a lens of fear, doubt, or limitation rather than possibility or hope.

For instance, you might find yourself questioning someone's intentions or getting caught in an anxious cycle, repeatedly checking to ensure you're not making mistakes. This thinking narrows your perspective, limits possibilities, and creates a distorted, negative view of life.

The first step in breaking free from this habit is recognizing it. Simply noticing that your mind has shifted toward unhelpful thoughts is the beginning of change. However, fighting or suppressing these thoughts doesn't work. Rather, it often adds more resistance, stress, and frustration.

Instead, shift your body and mind with simple Brain Sports activities. Take a walk around your neighborhood, try light body tapping, dance to your favorite music, or meditate. Pause to acknowledge, with gratitude, that you've noticed your mind drifting into negativity. Then, turn on your BrainPhone, focus on what you truly want, and take small, intentional steps toward your goals. Change won't happen overnight, but you can build this ability with consistent practice.

This ability to shift from negativity to positivity is essential, as positive emotions not only lift our mood but also broaden our thinking and reveal new possibilities. Research from the University of North Carolina found that participants who watched uplifting films that evoked emotions like joy and amusement generated more ideas than those who viewed films with a neutral or negative tone. This highlights how positive emotions can broaden our attention, opening our minds to new opportunities and fostering more creative, innovative thinking.

Positive thinking also directly affects your physical health. A study from Johns Hopkins University found that positive thinking significantly reduces the risk of heart disease, even for individuals with a family history of heart problems. In contrast, chronic negative thinking has been linked to an increased risk of dementia and Alzheimer's disease.

The most powerful form of positivity is "absolute positivity"—a mindset that doesn't rely on circumstances to determine your outlook. Absolute positivity doesn't mean ignoring life's challenges or pretending everything is fine when it's not. Instead, it is a steady inner strength that allows you to face life's difficulties with a calm, resilient perspective, no matter what comes your way.

Absolute positivity is not about blind optimism; it's about trusting in your ability to navigate any situation, no matter how difficult. It transcends a "can do" or "can't do" mindset and encourages the belief that, even if the gap between where you are and where you want to be seems wide, you can take steps to close it.

People with absolute positivity don't avoid problems; they face them head-on and use them as opportunities to grow and improve. They ask, "What opportunity exists here?" and take meaningful action to turn that opportunity into reality. This mindset focuses on solutions instead of problems and considers what can work rather than what can't. Absolute positivity fuels action by shifting your focus from passively reacting to circumstances to actively shaping them.

Cultivating absolute positivity requires consistent practice. Be patient and kind to yourself along the way. Avoid being overly critical—treat each experience as an opportunity to grow. Encourage yourself, accept setbacks as part of the process, and keep going. With consistent practice, your brain will gradually adapt to positive thinking, and positivity will become your natural state of mind over time.

The Gifts of Life

Some people believe, "Everything I have today is because of my hard work," but is that really true? Can we confidently say that our efforts alone created the life we have today? Looking more closely at the circumstances surrounding our lives, it becomes clear that individual effort alone cannot explain everything.

For instance, income level, one of the key determinants of quality of life, is heavily influenced by where a person is born rather than just their abilities or hard work. The difference in average income between someone born in the United States and someone born in a less developed country is so significant that no amount of effort alone can easily close that gap. According to 2024 statistics, the average GDP of the top 10 countries is about 35 times higher than that of the bottom 10 countries. While individual effort can narrow income gaps within a country, the disparity between countries is largely determined by factors outside one's control. In addition, the circumstances of the family we are born into, the social background of our parents, and the education and opportunities we receive also profoundly influence our lives.

This doesn't mean effort doesn't matter. We certainly have an incredible ability to improve and shape our lives through hard work and conscious choices. Thanks to neuroplasticity, our brains can adapt and change, and the mind has the power to push beyond limitations and create new opportunities. However, it's equally important to recognize that much of what we enjoy in life is not the result of our efforts alone. This realization shifts our perspective and gives us a deeper understanding of life.

We didn't choose when or where we were born, and we didn't choose the planet we live on. The people we've met and the opportunities we've received to learn and grow were not entirely of our design. Even the intricate wiring of our brains, which determines how we think and behave, is shaped by a lifetime of experiences and external influences. How much can we truly claim to have achieved solely through our own will or effort?

We cultivate a more profound sense of gratitude and humility when we acknowledge that many of life's circumstances, opportunities, and encounters are gifts. This perspective helps us recognize the value of what we have while opening our minds to new possibilities. It allows us to let go of the heavy burdens of perfectionism or the need to control everything, and it gives us the wisdom to distinguish between what is within our control and what is not.

By accepting this truth, we free ourselves from unnecessary worry and redirect our energy toward what truly matters. With this mindset, we can move forward with greater clarity, purpose, and peace, grounded in the understanding that life itself is a gift.

Be Grateful

When Newton discovered the principle of gravity, inspired by an apple falling from a tree, it marked a turning point in understanding the natural world. This breakthrough led many to view the universe as a precisely engineered clock operated by predictable mathematical laws. They believed that by studying and measuring these laws with enough accuracy, they could fully explain how the universe worked and even predict future events with certainty.

However, this mechanical view of the universe began to unravel. The discovery that time and space are not fixed but relative and that matter can exist as both particles and waves shattered the belief in a perfectly predictable universe. Science revealed that uncertainty isn't a rare exception but a fundamental property of the universe.

Scientific progress continues to accelerate today, teaching us more about the world and ourselves. Yet, the deeper we explore, the more we realize how much remains unknown. Theories such as Newton's law of gravity, Einstein's theory of relativity, and quantum mechanics were created by humans, but the natural laws and principles they describe have always existed. They were there long before we discovered them, silently shaping the universe.

The same is true of the technologies and devices we use. While humans design and build them, they rely on natural laws and principles that have always been part of the universe. From the smallest particles to solar systems and galaxies, everything we know, everything we will one day discover, and even the mysteries that remain beyond our reach are already at work in nature. These forces drive the phenomena we experience, the processes of life, and the world's constant evolution.

We are part of this vast, interconnected system, subject to the same laws and principles that govern all existence. Even a grain of sand or a single seed holds incredible wisdom and complexity far beyond what we can fully understand.

At the core of it all is energy—the fundamental force that drives the universe. Energy is in constant motion, never pausing, continuously creating and transforming everything around us. It is the source of life and mind connecting us to the infinite processes of creation and change that shape our world.

The life in our body and the mind we experience are just a small part of a much larger, interconnected existence. Our thoughts or knowledge do not allow us to be born, breathe, or move through the countless experiences and relationships in our lives. Beneath it all is the flow of energy that sustains and connects everything in the universe. This energy is the source of life, a force of deep wisdom and boundless love that keeps the world in motion.

We cannot fully understand or control this vast flow of energy, but we can learn to sense it and live in harmony with it. The thoughts we think, the words we speak, and the actions we take create ripples in this flow, interacting with other energies—sometimes in harmony, sometimes in tension. By paying attention to our inner feelings and becoming more aware of our energy, we can align ourselves with this flow, finding greater balance and clarity in our lives. By consciously regulating our own energy, we can also choose to live in harmony with others and the world around us, creating a more balanced and harmonious way of living.

Our lives are not sustained by our knowledge, abilities, or efforts alone but also by the goodwill and love of this energy. Understanding this is not about passively accepting life but gaining real wisdom. Realizing we have this support frees us from attachment and fear. Bolstered by this universal energy and mind, we can create our lives with purpose and clarity. Learning to trust energy is like learning to swim; we must relax into the feeling of buoyancy. Trusting the energy flow allows us to experience true freedom and peace. It inspires us to adopt an attitude of absolute positivity—not by comparing positives and negatives, but by embracing everything with genuine gratitude.

Our connection to this universal flow of energy not only shapes our present experiences but also influences how we navigate what lies ahead. Life is inherently unpredictable, and by learning to align with this ever-changing energy, we can approach challenges and opportunities with resilience and clarity.

The future is uncertain, but this is not a problem—it is a gift. Uncertainty makes life dynamic, meaningful, and full of potential. If everything were fixed and predictable, life would lose its sense of freedom, discovery, and growth.

Uncertainty holds possibilities—opportunities to learn and overcome challenges. The most effective way to guide these possibilities in the direction we desire is through positive expectations and gratitude. Positive expectations inspire hope and keep us focused on what is possible, while gratitude grounds us and gives us a sense of stability, even in difficult moments. Together, they allow us to feel like we are already experiencing the future we hope to create.

Gratitude is a stabilizing force that prevents us from being overwhelmed by negativity. When things don't go as planned, rather than falling into blame toward others or ourselves, ask, "What can I learn from this experience?" and appreciate the growth that comes from it. View unexpected challenges not as obstacles but as opportunities. Ask yourself, "What good can come from this?" and focus on finding value in the situation.

Gratitude and positive expectations are the most powerful tools for navigating an uncertain future. They help us transform fear of the unknown into excitement for what's possible. Rather than avoiding uncertainty, we can move forward with confidence and curiosity. Step fully into the unknown, trusting in the process of life, where you have the freedom to choose, create, learn, and grow. By working in harmony with the energy that drives all existence, we can turn uncertainty into opportunity and live with greater purpose, balance, and meaning.

Practices for Positivity and Gratitude

Practicing daily gratitude is one of the most impactful ways to clear your mind and maintain positive energy. By cultivating feelings of joy, appreciation, and openness, gratitude brings a sense of peace and helps you stay centered on what truly matters. To make gratitude a lasting habit, here are three practical ways to nurture positivity and transform your daily life.

SMILING PRACTICE

Smiling and laughing have a measurable impact on both physical and mental health. Laughter triggers the release of endorphins, which reduce stress, lift mood, and even alleviate pain. It also stimulates the release of dopamine and serotonin—chemicals that can ease depression, calm aggression, and promote mental balance, helping you develop a more positive outlook. On a physical level, laughter reduces the stress response, supports heart health, and strengthens your immune system. For example, it increases white blood cell production, which improves your body's ability to fight infections.

Beyond their health benefits, smiling and laughing are powerful tools for improving communication and building stronger relationships. A genuine smile or laugh can break down barriers, foster trust, and create a positive environment. This positive energy doesn't just affect those around us; it shifts our mindset, helping us see situations with greater clarity, optimism, and creativity.

However, smiling and laughing consistently isn't always easy. Daily stresses, negative environments, and social norms can make it challenging to express joy naturally. It takes intentional effort to build this habit, but it's worth it.

Here are two simple practices to help you make smiling and laughter a part of your daily life:

First, begin and end your day with gratitude and a smile. Spend one minute each morning when you wake up and one minute at night before going to sleep, smiling and reflecting on something you're grateful for. This small habit can set a positive tone for your entire day and help you wind down with a peaceful mind.

Second, pick one day each week to focus on smiling and laughing as much as possible. Remind yourself throughout the day, "I smile and laugh," and gently bring your attention back to it if you forget. This practice isn't forcing laughter—it's a way to reclaim control of your brain and mind. If outward smiling or laughter isn't appropriate, imagine a smile in your mind. Visualizing a smile can be surprisingly effective in shifting your energy and reducing stress.

By intentionally practicing smiling and laughter, you can create a positive ripple effect that improves your well-being, strengthens your relationships, and helps you handle life with more balance and optimism.

100 THINGS TO BE GRATEFUL FOR

Take a moment to write down the things you are grateful for. It could be anything—an object, a memory, a relationship, your talents, or even small moments in your day. It could be the cup of coffee in front of you, a tree branch swaying in the wind, or the smile of a loved one.

Through this exercise, you will realize how many blessings and opportunities you have already received and how many of them you may have taken for granted. This is your chance to rediscover the meaning and value of those overlooked moments.

If possible, write 100 things you are grateful for. If writing 100 things at once feels overwhelming, break it into smaller steps by writing 10 things daily for 10 days. To make it easier, focus on a specific theme each day. For example, you could reflect on loved ones who support and care for you, the opportunities your work provides, the small joys that bring peace and happiness to your day, the beauty of nature that nurtures your spirit, or the talents and personal growth that enrich your life.

Once you have made your list, read it aloud and say, "Thank you" for each item. Read slowly, savoring the meaning behind every word, and allow gratitude to fill your heart. Take your time—this is not a task to rush. After you have expressed appreciation for the 10 items you wrote that day, close your eyes and focus on your heart. Let the feeling of gratitude rise from deep within you. Fully immerse yourself in that feeling, staying with it for a while.

The true power of this practice lies in repetition. Instead of doing it just once, practice it every day for at least a week, and ideally, make it a part of your daily routine. Each day, as you express gratitude, it will take a deeper root in your mind and heart. Over time, you will naturally become more aware of the blessings around you and experience a positive shift in your outlook and overall perspective on life.

If you ever find your feelings of gratitude fading, revisit the list you have written. Reading it again can rekindle those feelings of appreciation and remind you of the abundance already present in your life. Creating a new list to reflect fresh blessings or new experiences can also renew your sense of gratitude.

If you feel grateful to someone, don't hesitate to express it. A simple act—a heartfelt phone call, a thoughtful text, an email, or a kind word shared face-to-face—can make a profound difference. Your words of appreciation can brighten their day, strengthen your bond, and inspire a ripple of positivity. Gratitude grows when shared, and expressing it uplifts others and fills your life with greater joy, warmth, and connection.

ACCEPTANCE AND APPRECIATION DAY

Choose one day a week to practice unconditional acceptance and gratitude. This doesn't mean ignoring real danger or putting up with unfair treatment. It means intentionally avoiding knee-jerk reactions of resistance—those automatic thoughts or feelings of "no"—to the experiences you encounter. Setting aside just one day a week for this practice allows you to observe your reactions more clearly and focus on shifting your perspective.

Today, notice how often you react negatively to things that don't match your ideas, preferences, or habits. These reactions happen so quickly that they often go unnoticed, yet they steer your thoughts, emotions, and actions while shutting out other possibilities. Many disagreements, frustrations, and conflicts start from these split-second reactions.

The practice is simple: accept every situation or experience without rushing to label it as good or bad, positive or negative. Instead, ask yourself, "What's good about this?" This question helps you pause, look more closely, and find something positive, even in challenging situations. From there, decide on the most constructive and thoughtful action you can take, and carry it out.

Dedicating one full day to this practice is important because it's hard to notice your reaction patterns when you're on autopilot. By observing your responses for a single day, you'll understand how you interact with life's challenges and develop the ability to respond with more awareness and balance.

This realization can also be applied to the day of smiling practice introduced earlier. By choosing a specific day to focus on smiling, you'll become more aware of when you're not smiling and take steps to shift your mood. Whether it's acceptance or smiling, focusing on these practices for just one day helps you build awareness and make small, meaningful changes that can ripple through your life.

* * *

The above practices create the emotional and energetic environment for your brain to function at its best. They cultivate acceptance, gratitude, and positivity as second nature, transforming how you perceive and experience life. These practices help you recognize opportunities, connect with positive energy, and deepen your appreciation for life as a gift.

With Brain Sports, such as mindful movement, meditation, and creative activities, you reinforce these positive patterns, integrating them into your daily routine. As gratitude and positivity become part of your everyday life, even greater blessings and joy will naturally flow into it.

When you encounter uncertainty, don't avoid it. Instead, welcome it with positive expectations, gratitude, and purposeful action. As you do, you will realize how much of a gift life truly is and how the universe is always working with you, guiding you, and helping to fulfill your wishes.

CHAPTER 11

MEET THE DIVINE IN THE BRAIN

On a small farm in New Zealand, I watched my golden retriever give birth to a litter of puppies. She was less than two years old and gave birth to 10 puppies. When it was time, the mother dog found a safe place for herself and settled in.

After each pup was born, she carefully cut the umbilical cord and licked the amniotic fluid to clean it. Afterward, she ate the placenta to replenish her energy and regain her strength. The puppies, without any guidance, instinctively searched for their mother's body to nurse and sustain their lives. No one taught the mother dog how to give birth and care for her pups, and the pups were never taught how to find milk. They were following an innate wisdom, life's guidance built into their nature.

Watching the birth of the golden retrievers, I felt deeply connected to the presence of God. I saw how life unfolds with wisdom far more significant than anything we can consciously grasp. I've never met God face-to-face, never heard a voice declare, "I am God." Yet, I feel a profound certainty of God's existence—a natural law, an energy, a life force that governs the world.

Nature follows an inherent order and flow, finding harmony and balance amid constant change. This ability is present in all living things. It's evident in how the Earth revolves around the sun at the perfect distance, how tree roots grow deep into the soil in search of water, and how birds navigate the skies on the wind.

This flow ensures the sun rises every morning, rivers continue their course, and oceans stay in motion. It's a force that connects everything, from the smallest particle to the vast universe, creating a seamless web of interconnection. This force—this natural energy and wisdom—is what I understand as universal energy and universal mind. To me, this is God. It is a force that sustains life, present in the rhythms of nature and woven into everything around us.

This force is not only around us. It's within us. A baby's heart begins to beat on its own at birth, and our breath continues unconsciously, sustaining us moment by moment. When we are injured, our bodies start healing on their own. At night, sleep overtakes us, restoring our minds and bodies. We often believe we are the ones sustaining our lives through our efforts, yet the truth is that we do not earn the most essential aspects of life—they are gifts. They unfold naturally, guided by the divine workings within our bodies and minds, the laws of nature, and the profound wisdom of life itself.

In truth, nothing in this world isn't connected to this force. Whether we realize it or not, every moment is an encounter with what I call God. But many people see God as something outside themselves, a transcendent entity to be found only in specific places, like temples or churches. Some believe that understanding God's will requires scripture or religious doctrine. Others think they must rely on a particular prophet or belief system to connect with God, fearing losing favor if they stray.

However, thinking of God as something external and accessible only through specific methods or persons can feel limiting and unsettling. This discomfort deepens when we consider needing restrictions or particular conditions to connect with God. It becomes even more troubling when we imagine God as favoring certain groups while rejecting others. This discomfort is not accidental. It reflects a deeper truth within us. It's the voice of the divine, naturally and intuitively guiding us. It's not something learned or taught; it's an inherent awareness. This inner signal tells us that such limiting ideas do not align with the true nature of God. God is not confined to particular places, scriptures, or traditions. God exists in everything and everyone.

This inner sense—this resonance, wisdom, and intuitive knowing—arises from the same life force that guides all of nature. It is the action of the divine, the essence of divinity within us. This is what the BrainPhone ultimately seeks to access and amplify.

At the Heart of Humanity Is Divinity

My conviction that God resides within every person is deeply rooted in my own experience, because that is the reality of God as I have felt it. At the end of a 21-day solo meditation on Mount Moak in South Korea, where I searched for answers to the questions, "Who am I?" and "What is the meaning of life?" I had an experience that completely transformed my life. I heard a powerful sound within my brain as if it resonated from both inside me and the sky above. It felt as though the entire universe was filled with nothing but the vibration of that sound. I heard: "Universal energy is my energy, and my energy is universal energy. Universal mind is my mind, and my mind is universal mind."

At that moment, I realized that the energy within my body and the energy flowing through the universe were not separate. They were one. I understood that my mind and the mind of the universe, which I think of as God's mind, were not separate. This realization came not as intellectual knowledge or language but as an energetic knowing that resonated through my entire being.

As this awareness dawned, the boundaries between my body and the outside world seemed to dissolve. My energy and mind expanded to fill the entire universe. The pulse of the cosmos became one with my pulse, and I experienced the universe breathing through me, its heartbeat pulsing within me. I didn't just think about God at that moment. I felt God. What I experienced was not an abstract idea but the eternal life force itself. As I experienced it, God is *eternal life that exists alone and on its own.*

It is alone because it is the source of all things, containing everything, with nothing existing outside of it. It is on its own because it owes its being to no external cause. It is eternal, without beginning or end, never having been created and never ceasing to exist. God is life itself: a boundless, eternal flow of energy vibrating with infinite creative possibilities.

What makes this understanding truly profound is the realization that God's essence is also mine. I am that eternal life, existing alone and on its own. I am limitless and formless, and I have complete energy and life capable of creating and embracing everything. This realization struck me with an overwhelming sense of awe and exhilaration.

Even more profoundly, I realized this truth wasn't just about me. It applies to everyone. The eternal life that exists alone and on its own isn't unique to me but is present in every person. In other words, the essence of God is in all of us.

The values we hold as the highest—the most divine, infinite, loving, and wisdom-filled source of creation that we call "God"—are not separate from us. They live within each of us, making every human being inherently worthy and valuable. Recognizing that everyone shares the same divine essence reshapes how we see ourselves and others. It reminds us of our profound connection, infinite worth, and sacred nature.

I believe humanity's spiritual masters, both those we know and those yet to be discovered, have experienced something similar to what I have experienced as God. At their core, I don't think these experiences are different, regardless of spiritual tradition.

The key message these spiritual masters wanted to share was understanding an eternal life that exists alone and on its own—a universal truth that resides within everyone. They sought to show that this realization wasn't something unique to them but something we all have the potential to discover. Through their journeys, they hoped to inspire others to recognize this truth within themselves and connect with the divine life that unites us all.

Over time, the spiritual teachings of these masters became entangled in organized religions and rigid doctrines. Instead of directly experiencing the essence of their message—the life and divinity within themselves—people began to focus on following the teachers or the institutions built around their teachings.

This shift led many to abandon a personal connection with the divine, preventing them from truly experiencing God. They emphasized external rules and practices more than the inner truth these teachings were meant to inspire. I believe connecting to God truly means looking within ourselves, just as humanity's spiritual masters did. They discovered God within themselves, and I think we can do the same.

God is not something we need to learn about or study. It is something we can experience and feel. God is not a being to worship from a distance but something we can embody in our lives. It's not an external force to search for but a presence already within us, ready to be realized and expressed.

The Brain as a Gateway to the Divine

This idea is beautifully articulated in the *Chun Bu Kyung*, an ancient Korean scripture. Unlike texts that focus on teaching about good and evil, the *Chun Bu Kyung* conveys, in just 81 characters, the origins of the universe, its workings, and the nature of humanity.

One passage describes the divine within us this way: "Our mind is as bright as the sun, and when it is illuminated, heaven and earth become one in human." This insight suggests that our minds share the same brightness as the divine. We can become one with the divine by recognizing and realizing this truth within ourselves.

Another passage from the *Samil Shingo*, another ancient Korean scripture, deeply resonates with me. It states: "Find God in your own nature. It already descended in your brain." This message emphasizes that the essence of God is already within us—specifically, within our brains. It's fascinating that, more than 5,000 years ago, people understood that humans could experience the divine through their brains, even without the knowledge of modern neuroscience. This understanding likely came from their intuitive insights and direct experiences.

We don't need to search for the divine outside of ourselves; the essence of the divine is already within our minds. We can experience this connection through the brain. Even the feeling of connecting with the divine in a sacred place or the beauty of nature is shaped by our brain. The longing to connect with the divine, as well as the recognition of that connection, also arises from the brain.

I believe the most critical value of the human brain is its ability to help us discover the divine within ourselves. Likewise, the greatest purpose of being human is to realize that divinity and become God itself. The essence of humanity is divinity, and the core of what it means to be a person is the realization of this inner divinity.

I recognize that this statement may lead to misunderstandings. When I talk about God, I'm not referring to an all-powerful being that transcends physical limitations or controls everything, as some religious traditions describe. Instead, I am referring to our spiritual potential—the capacity for infinite creativity and wisdom, unconditional compassion, and boundless love.

By reclaiming the potential of our brains, we uncover our true humanity and take a step toward living more meaningful, impactful lives. This is the ultimate purpose of Brain Sports and activating the BrainPhone: to transcend limitations and experience life as a reflection of universal energy and wisdom. Connecting with this divine flow unlocks the brain's highest function, guiding us on the journey to brain glory, where our spiritual potential fully blossoms, radiating creativity, love, and boundless possibility.

Pathways to the Divine Energy

Meditation is the most effective way to experience the divine through the brain. Beyond relaxing the body and mind, meditation allows you to observe your inner world more clearly. It awakens observer consciousness—the part of you that notices your thoughts, emotions, and sensations from a calm, detached perspective.

This awakened state enables you to see your feelings and thoughts as temporary experiences rather than being controlled by them. As observer consciousness develops, it enhances your self-awareness and mindful presence. Many practical benefits of meditation, such as greater stress tolerance, improved resilience, and sharper clarity and focus, arise from cultivating this powerful state of awareness.

As meditation deepens, observer consciousness takes us into a more profound experience. Over time, the line between the observer and the observed begins to fade. For example, the sense that we are watching our emotions, thoughts, or breath gradually disappears, and it feels like we become the breath itself. It is as if all the experiences and sensations within us merge into one continuous flow of energy, and we feel like a single vibration, one energy, moving within a cosmic flow. At this point, the distinction between observer and observed disappears, and we are no longer the observer but the experience itself.

One word that describes what many people experience in this meditative state is "oneness." In this state, you don't just understand. You deeply feel with your whole body that you, the universe, and everything around you are connected. You realize that everything is moving together as part of the same flow of energy and consciousness.

In this state of unity, the passage of time seems to vanish. The moment stretches infinitely, and you feel yourself dissolving into the eternal now. Anxiety, worry, and fear fade, replaced by a profound sense of peace, stillness, and stability. The heavy emotions that once weighed you down dissipate, making space for feelings of infinite love, peace, and freedom. You also feel connected to limitless potential and strength, free from boundaries or restrictions. This sense of unity brings a feeling of being deeply connected to everything around you in complete harmony.

This is the state described in the *Chun Bu Kyung* as the mind illuminated as bright as the sun and in the *Samil Shingo* as the mind encountering God descended in the brain. It is the state of experiencing the eternal life that exists alone and on its own. At this moment, our mind merges with the mind of the universe, and our energy unites with the universe's energy. It is a state of complete unity, where the mind fully knows itself, energy deeply feels itself, and life wholly experiences life itself. This is the moment of encountering God as the energy of the universe and the Great Life Force.

For those new to meditation, this description might sound like a supernatural experience straight out of a superhero movie. Beginners who find it challenging to focus because of distractions might see it as an idea far removed from their own experience. However, reaching this state of unity is not as difficult as it may seem. With consistent practice, anyone can feel a sense of connection and oneness with the divine.

There are many meditation methods available, and many of them can help you experience a sense of unity with the divine. From my practice and teaching meditation to many people, I've found that energy meditation is one of the most effective ways to feel the divine within yourself.

Energy meditation involves directly sensing and experiencing the subtle energy that flows within and around your body. While most people are not usually aware of this energy, with practice, anyone can develop the ability to feel it.

When you activate your energy centers using techniques like breathing, qigong, vibrational exercises, or sound, your energy senses awaken. You might feel energy flowing from your fingertips or toes or notice areas of your body becoming warm or vibrating. These sensations often expand, creating a feeling that your body is connected to the space around you. This clear and direct experience reveals how you are part of a larger energy field beyond your physical boundaries.

At first, you may intentionally guide and work with this energy, but over time, it flows naturally, leading you into a deeper sense of unity. As this experience deepens, the boundaries of self start to dissolve, and your mind and body feel as though they are expanding infinitely, merging with the energy of the universe. This creates a profound sense of oneness and connection.

Why Unity with the Divine Matters

Experiencing unity with the divine is transformative, not just because of the stillness, peace, or deep sense of security it brings in the moment, but because it allows us to understand our true nature and inspires us to create positive change in ourselves and the world.

We often identify ourselves with our thoughts, feelings, and experiences: our personality, strengths, weaknesses, successes, failures, what we have, and what we lack. But when we experience unity with the divine, we begin to see that these are just parts of who we are—they don't define our essence.

In those moments of divine unity, we recognize ourselves as whole and infinite beings rather than individuals limited by the challenges we face. Anxiety, pain, and even joy become temporary states while our true essence exists beyond them. We realize that we are life itself, filled with infinite love, creativity, and wisdom.

This understanding creates a significant shift: we see that external achievements or circumstances don't determine our worth. Success doesn't make us more valuable, nor does failure make us less so. Our worth isn't something we earn—it has always been within us, and it continues to shine. With this awareness, we know, deep down, that we are entirely worthy just as we are, incomparable to anything else.

From this understanding, we can declare with conviction, "I am me! I am who I am." This realization of our unchanging essence frees us from comparing ourselves to others and feeling inadequate or superior. It helps us develop deep love and trust in ourselves, allowing us to live with greater peace and authenticity, guided by our inner voice instead of external judgments.

When we understand that our essence is love and creativity, we also begin to see these qualities in others. This leads to deeper empathy, trust, and compassion for all living beings. From this awareness grows a *Hongik* heart—a genuine desire to act in ways that benefit everyone, not just ourselves.

Experiencing unity with the divine also helps us see new possibilities and take charge of our lives. When we realize that our essence is infinite creativity, yesterday's failures no longer hold us back from trying something new today. Obstacles or limitations are no longer reasons to give up on our dreams. Instead, we find the strength to renew ourselves daily and bring fresh energy and purpose to our lives.

This deep connection with the divine also allows us to recognize the sacred in ordinary moments. In the morning sunlight that signals a new day for all life, in the steady presence of a tree that provides clean air, or in a glass of water that has traveled through the atmosphere to nourish us—we can feel the divine energy that sustains everything.

We also find this divine presence in a child's curious eyes, a mother's gentle touch as she cradles her child, or the small kindness of a stranger holding a door open. Through meditation, the experience of unity with the divine helps us see these everyday moments in a new light, making them richer and more meaningful, and filling our lives with a sense of spiritual depth and fulfillment.

The Value of Energy Experiences

I have shared my belief that divinity represents the highest potential of the human brain and explained why energy meditation is one of the most direct ways to experience the divine. This is why practicing feeling and working with energy is at the core of every Brain Education method I teach. But there is another reason why I value energy experiences so much.

The previously mentioned *Chun Bu Kyung* states, "All things begin with One, but that One has no beginning," and, "All things end with One, but that One has no end." These verses teach that this One, which has no beginning and no end, is the essence of everything that exists. This One represents God, life, and our true selves.

These teachings emphasize the concept of oneness, transcending all boundaries and dichotomies such as beginning and end, matter and spirit, or good and evil. Unlike approaches that focus on dualities, the philosophy of *Chun Bu Kyung* centers on the One as the ultimate reality that encompasses and unifies all things. This One is not limited by opposites or divisions but is the essence of everything. It offers a perspective that goes beyond conventional binary thinking.

It's hard to fully grasp oneness through conceptual thinking, which tends toward contrasting, categorization, and abstraction. Also, a mindset that divides matter and consciousness, mind and body, into separate categories cannot lead to understanding that which lies beyond. Instead, I believe that the key to experiencing oneness beyond these divisions lies in "energy."

Energy is neither matter nor consciousness, yet it can encompass both. It is neither body nor mind, but it can contain both. Energy has no opposites or contradictions—it is unifying and all-encompassing. When you experience energy, there's no need to analyze or intellectually understand it. You simply feel it in your body and mind. You intuitively know, through the vibrations of energy and sensations in your body, that everything is one.

In this experience of oneness, you feel an immense love for all things. This love has no conditions or reasons—it simply exists. In this state, the ego fades away, and human divisions and boundaries disappear. Whether caused by us or others, wounds and pain dissolve, leaving a renewed sense of love and hope for ourselves, humanity, and all life.

Energy led me to my most profound spiritual insights, and modern physics reveals that energy is also the foundation of existence. Energy bridges spirituality and science, showing us that these two realms are not as separate as they might seem.

For these reasons, I believe a worldview rooted in energy can help heal and integrate the dualistic thinking and conflicts underlying many of our society's challenges. This worldview isn't new—it has deep roots in many spiritual traditions, and energy has long been a key framework for understanding the world in East Asia. Energy has been applied to many areas of life, including martial arts, medicine, art, and personal development. By embracing this energy-centered perspective, we can create a healthier and more harmonious way of living that nurtures our bodies and minds, strengthens our relationships, and fosters harmony with nature. This is why I believe it's so important for everyone to learn how to sense and work with energy.

Eternal Life Beyond Death

Death is a reality that everyone will face, and for many, it brings fear and uncertainty. But those who come to understand the deeper nature of life see death differently. They recognize that life is not confined to the physical body and find peace in the knowledge that existence continues beyond what we perceive as the end.

At its core, our essence is divinity and energy, eternal and unending. Life and death are like a light bulb turning on and off. We come alive when energy flows into the body, just as a bulb lights up. When the energy leaves, life departs, like the bulb going dark. Yet, just as electricity doesn't vanish when the light goes out, life energy doesn't disappear. It moves beyond the physical form.

From the perspective of life energy, there is no life or death. The energy expressed through a physical body is called life, while death returns energy to its larger flow. It's like water freezing into ice or evaporating into steam—the form changes, but the essence remains the same.

When we understand this principle, we realize that death is not the end but a transition. Life and death are not opposites but different expressions of the same infinite flow. On a physical level, death exists, but on an energetic and spiritual level, it is a natural shift, much like the seasons changing or the wind coming and going.

All life shares this universal cycle. We arise from a greater energy source and return to it, an unbroken flow with neither beginning nor end. Eternal life isn't about reaching a specific place, like heaven or hell, nor is it necessarily about reincarnation. Instead, it's about recognizing the eternal nature of the energy that animates us.

The fear of death often arises from the belief that we will cease to exist entirely—that we, along with everything and everyone we cherish, will be lost forever. This fear can feel overwhelming. However, understanding the nature of eternal life transforms this perspective at its root. The fear begins to fade when we recognize that life and death are part of the same continuous flow. We come to see that nothing truly disappears; it simply changes form.

This understanding can transform how we live. When we let go of the fear of death, we gain the courage to face life's challenges and opportunities confidently. We can live more freely, more fully, and with greater appreciation for each moment. Life becomes an experience of deep trust and gratitude, rooted in the understanding that our existence is part of the eternal flow of energy. By embracing this perspective, we connect more deeply with the present and live with a profound sense of purpose and peace.

Three Practices to Awaken Inner Divinity

Recognizing that our essence is inherently divine is not just an abstract concept but something we can experience directly through energy meditation. When we connect with our divinity, we take an important step toward fulfilling our spiritual potential. Here are three grounded practices to help you experience this connection through energy.

ENERGY DANCE TO MOVE WITH LIFE'S FLOW

Energy Dance, or *Dahnmu*, is a meditative practice that helps you connect with your body and the energy within you. It allows you to move naturally and freely, guided by the flow of energy, creating a sense of unity and connection with the divinity within.

Start by preparing your body with a simple relaxation technique, such as Shaking Meditation or Brain Wave Vibration. Once you feel calm, sit in a chair or on the floor and begin an energy-sensing meditation. Place your palms facing each other in front of your chest, then slowly move them closer together and farther apart. Focus on the sensation between your hands, letting the energy build without forcing the motion. Let this growing sensation express itself freely, allowing your inner feelings to flow with the movement.

Then, permit your body to follow the movements of your hands naturally without judgment. As the energy flows through your arms, shoulders, and torso, your movements may become larger and more fluid. Let the energy extend to your head, hips, legs, and feet, allowing your entire body to move freely. If you feel the urge to stand, follow it, and let your body express itself fully.

The dance can take many forms. It may sometimes feel gentle and serene, like a flower swaying gracefully in a soft breeze. Other times, it may become intense and powerful, like thunder and lightning during a stormy night. Your body might vibrate, stretch, or move unexpectedly, and you may even make unfamiliar sounds. Instead of holding back or suppressing these expressions, embrace them without reservation and give your body the freedom to express itself authentically without restraint.

As you move, thoughts and emotions might arise. Step back and observe these feelings without judgment, letting them flow through you without taking control. This practice helps you experience emotions fully while remaining grounded. It also allows you to cultivate the emotions you want to feel.

Gradually, you may notice a shift in your experience of the energy. At first, you might guide the movements intentionally, but gradually, the energy will take the lead, expressing itself freely through your body. In this state, you experience a profound sense of unity—your body, mind, and energy flowing as one.

This soulful connection resonates through every cell in your body, often bringing tears of joy or release. Energy Dance is a transformative practice that allows you to rediscover your true essence while cultivating a deep sense of inner harmony and freedom.

SOUL SINGING TO EXPRESS INNER HARMONY

Sound is a powerful tool for transforming our feelings because it is vibration at its core. While music, instruments, and other tools can help, the most direct way to use sound is with our own voice. The vibrations we create with our voice resonate throughout our body and mind, creating a natural shift in our energy from the inside out.

This practice doesn't require following a set pitch or rhythm; instead, it's about letting your feelings guide you. Start by closing your eyes and focusing on your chest. Make long vowel sounds such as "ah," "oh," and "ooh." Once you feel comfortable, experiment by adding notes to these sounds. Rather than try to sing a familiar melody, allow yourself to create something entirely your own. Let go of overthinking and simply listen to your voice. When you tune in to the feelings in your heart and express them through sound, your voice flows naturally and authentically. It becomes uniquely yours, a personal expression that no one else can replicate.

There's no need to aim for specific pitches or beats and no judgment involved. The goal is to express yourself freely, following your inner sense of what feels right. As you continue, your pitch, rhythm, and intensity will naturally adjust to create a sound that feels good. The key is to make sounds that feel comfortable and soothing for you to hear.

Your brain is naturally wired to find balance and harmony. As you sing freely, your brain will refine the sounds you create, helping you feel more grounded and secure. Everyone's voice has a unique rhythm and vibration, and when you sing authentically, you express your individuality. Even if your voice isn't polished like a professional singer's, the balance and harmony of your natural sound can still be deeply moving and beautiful.

This practice allows you to connect with your voice in a way that feels personal and freeing, like the sense of connection you might feel during Energy Dance. Spontaneous, free singing can be a powerful experience that balances your inner vibration and reorganizes scattered energy. It creates an opportunity to feel truly connected—to your life, your soul, and the divine within.

GETTING IN TOUCH WITH NATURE

The divine is nature's energy and life force that brings everything in the world to life. One simple way to connect with this presence is by spending time in nature. We are naturally drawn to nature because it is our origin. Like salmon returning to their home streams, we instinctively long for the embrace of the natural world, seeking comfort and a sense of belonging.

Nature doesn't communicate through words but speaks clearly in its own way, through silence, sensations, and the vibrations of life. It shows us things as they are, free from deception or pretense. There's no need to study or analyze when we're in nature; we simply feel and connect. This connection awakens something deep within us, stripping away the layers of artificial knowledge and information that often obscure our inner clarity and wisdom.

What we consider good or bad is often shaped by societal norms and changes with time, culture, and perspective. Nature, however, operates beyond these constructs. It doesn't judge us or compare us to others. In nature, there's no right or wrong, no good or evil. A flower blooms and fades, a leaf falls, and a river flows, all without judgment. This absence of labels can lighten the weight of societal expectations, helping us find peace and freedom in simply being.

Nature exists on its own terms. Rivers find their way to the ocean, and trees grow without instructions. We are part of this natural world; when we spend time in nature, we tap into the same self-sustaining power. It reminds us of our autonomy and our innate ability to grow, adapt, and thrive.

Connecting with nature is as simple as opening your heart. Walk among towering trees that have witnessed centuries, swim in the ocean, and feel the vitality of the water teeming with life.

Lie under the night sky and let the twinkling stars remind you of the vastness of existence. These moments don't require effort or explanation—just presence.

In nature's embrace, we rediscover how free and limitless we are. It teaches us through feeling rather than knowledge that all life is interwoven. Nature offers a pure and direct way to connect with the essence of life and its inherent divinity.

CHAPTER 12

A WORLD OF EVERYDAY SAGES

Today, life goals are often closely tied to career aspirations. From an early age, children are asked, "What do you want to be when you grow up?" with the expectation of answers like doctor, lawyer, businessperson, engineer, athlete, or entertainer. For adults, "What do you do?" is a frequent conversation starter, reflecting how strongly our occupations are connected to our sense of identity.

This career-focused mindset, however, is relatively modern. In traditional societies, life's purpose was not centered on professional success. For example, work was necessary in agrarian communities to sustain life, but it wasn't considered the primary meaning of life. Instead, greater importance was placed on maintaining strong family relationships, cooperating with others in the community, and living in harmony with the natural world.

In many traditional cultures, the foundation of a meaningful life rests on moral values and spiritual growth. Eastern philosophy, for instance, emphasized living in alignment with virtue and the Tao—a way of life focused on balance and harmony within oneself and with the universe. In Confucian thought, the ultimate goal was to become a "noble person," someone who cultivates self-discipline, acts with integrity, and contributes to the well-being of family and society. Similarly, many traditional societies aimed to develop individuals with strong moral characters who could positively impact their communities and the world.

Western traditions also reflected these values. In ancient Greece, philosophers like Aristotle taught that a meaningful life involved practicing virtue by seeking what is good for oneself and the community through reason and wisdom. In ancient Rome, Stoic philosophers such as Marcus Aurelius and Seneca believed that living in harmony with nature and cultivating inner calm and resilience were essential for leading a balanced and purposeful life.

Both Eastern and Western traditions viewed work as a means to an end rather than the central purpose of life. Instead, life's meaning was found in values such as cultivating virtue, living in harmony with nature, fostering inner peace, and contributing to the community.

Redefining Success: From Careers to Character

With the rise of industrialization and capitalism, careers have become a primary measure of social success and personal value. Life goals have shifted away from holistic values toward professional achievements. While careers provide structure, purpose, and financial stability, focusing too heavily on professional achievements can overlook other fundamental human needs for love, connection, and personal growth, leaving many feeling unfulfilled despite their accomplishments.

Moreover, centering life around "what do I do" is becoming an increasingly unstable foundation. Advances in technology, particularly AI, are rapidly reshaping society and the job market. Many roles are already being replaced or redefined, and this trend is accelerating. It is becoming less feasible to sustain a single career over an entire lifetime. In this environment, relying solely on professional success for identity and purpose is risky. When a job changes or disappears, it can profoundly shake one's sense of self and direction.

In a world marked by constant change and uncertainty, it is more important than ever to have an internal compass—a sense of identity and values that provide stability regardless of external circumstances. Shifting life goals from career-focused to character-focused is not just a philosophical ideal but a practical necessity. We must go beyond the question, "What am I going to do?" and ask the more profound, more enduring question, "Who am I going to be?" When we define the kind of person we want to become, the answers to "What am I going to do?" naturally become clearer and more meaningful.

AI has revolutionized work, but it cannot replace the unique human qualities that define our character and relationships. While AI can analyze data, mimic emotional responses, and perform even creative tasks, it cannot truly feel or understand human experiences. It cannot empathize with others' emotions, experience the inner pull of conscience to make moral choices, or ask questions about purpose and existence. On the other hand, humans are naturally driven to ask, "Who am I?" and, through that inquiry, find clarity about their values, essence, and life direction.

These character qualities—empathy, conscience, and self-reflection—are valuable for professional success and essential for leading a fulfilling life. In the future, jobs will no longer define our identity. Instead, life goals will expand to prioritize inner growth, meaningful relationships, and contributions to the community. Jobs may come and go, but our character and humanity remain constant. The most enduring way to live is to ask, "What kind of person do I want to be?" and intentionally design a life that reflects that vision.

Sages of Our Time

The question, "What kind of person do I want to be?" has answers that vary from individual to individual and can evolve with time and culture. However, at the core of human character lie universal values not bound by circumstances or the passage of time, as they stem from our shared nature. In this light, I propose sagehood as a practical and meaningful aspiration for everyone. Sagehood can be a goal we hold in our hearts and work toward throughout our lives.

When I speak to young children, I encourage them to "dream of becoming a sage." I explain that sages are some of the world's kindest, wisest, and most inspiring people. Their eyes light up excitedly, and they often respond enthusiastically, "I want to be a sage too!" With pre-teens, I adjust the message slightly, saying,

"Make becoming a sage your main goal, and let everything else you want to achieve support that." They usually smile and nod, finding the idea relatable and motivating.

However, when I share this idea with adults, the response is often skeptical. Many dismiss sagehood as unrealistic or overly idealistic. This skepticism likely stems from misconceptions about what it means to be a sage and deeply ingrained stereotypes portraying sages as figures far removed from ordinary life.

For many, the word *sage* evokes images of extraordinary figures like Jesus, Buddha, Confucius, or Muhammad—great teachers of humanity who are often portrayed as morally perfect, endlessly forgiving, and free of flaws. In some traditions, sages are viewed as beings with supernatural powers, entirely removed from the challenges and imperfections of everyday people. With such idealized images, it's no surprise that becoming a sage feels unattainable or even inappropriate for most people.

This idealized image creates a sense of separation. Ordinary people who make mistakes, have regrets, and sometimes act selfishly find it hard to imagine themselves as potential sages. Sages are often seen as figures to revere and admire rather than as examples to follow or ideals to aspire to. As a result, many people never even consider the possibility of striving to become a sage.

But why can't you or I aspire to sagehood? It's neither forbidden nor impossible. As I've emphasized, we all possess divinity within us. The rarity of sagehood throughout history may not reflect its inherent difficulty but rather the fact that many people have never dared to imagine it as a possibility or recognize it within themselves.

A sage is not a flawless moral figure or someone with extraordinary powers beyond reach. A sage in today's world is simply someone who recognizes the divinity within themselves, embraces the empathy, conscience, and altruism that arise from it, and strives to live out these qualities. In essence, a sage is a person who takes responsibility for themselves and their role in the world, expressing love and care through their actions. Isn't this the kind of sage we can all aspire to be? And isn't this the kind of sage we should encourage one another to become?

The Seeds of Sagehood

I believe everyone has the potential to become a sage because the seeds of sagehood exist within us all. However, these seeds do not grow independently—they require conscious effort and deliberate practice to nurture them and bring them to full maturity.

The Chinese philosopher Mencius famously said that every person has a heart that cannot bear to see others suffer. He illustrated this idea by saying, "When we see a child about to fall into a well, we feel a sense of alarm and compassion. This feeling does not arise because we wish to gain favor with the child's parents, to seek praise from others, or to establish a good reputation. It arises simply because we have a heart that cannot bear to see others suffer."

This compassionate heart that Mencius described is the seed of sagehood. It reflects our innate capacity for conscience, empathy, love, and the natural desire to help others. This is why we instinctively want to assist someone in need, check on a car stopped by the roadside, or rescue a shivering puppy in the rain.

It's also why we feel compelled to help people suffering from a natural disaster, even if we have no personal connection to them. These actions don't arise from calculated self-interest but from a natural flow of goodwill and care for others.

Modern neuroscience supports this idea by showing that our brains are wired to empathize with the pain and emotions of others. For example, when someone burns themselves by touching something hot, the pain they feel activates the same areas in the brain as someone watching it happen. This demonstrates that we're not just imagining someone else's pain; we're experiencing it alongside them on a neurological level. Our brains are fundamentally designed for deep connection with others.

Moreover, our brains are built to feel joy when we help others. Acts of kindness trigger the release of dopamine, a neurotransmitter associated with pleasure, creating a feeling similar to the satisfaction of enjoying a good meal or other positive experiences. However, the joy from altruistic acts goes deeper, providing a lasting sense of psychological well-being. Research shows that people who regularly engage in acts of kindness and altruism have lower stress levels, better physical health, and reduced rates of depression and anxiety compared to those who don't.

These findings underscore that humans are biologically wired to find meaning through connection and compassion. Our brains are naturally equipped to support sagehood. Empathy, conscience, love, and a benevolent heart are not extraordinary traits but intrinsic parts of our nature—the seeds of sagehood within us all. Becoming a sage doesn't mean striving for something unattainable; it means embracing and living the potential we are born with.

Turn on Sagehood Mode

Every day, we are surrounded by serious news. Wars, violence, and political conflicts dominate the headlines. Instead of respecting each other's differences and seeking solutions, conflicts often escalate as people defend their positions without compromise. This reality can leave many feeling frustrated and powerless.

It's natural to feel discomfort when witnessing discord and conflict. That discomfort reflects the seed of divinity and sagehood within us—a part of us that desires peace and harmony. If the state of the world bothers you and you feel compelled to reduce the conflict, you've already awakened the sage in you. It's not just a complaint; it's a manifestation of the peace-seeking nature deep within you.

If you feel anger and sadness when you see people suffering from war or violence, or a sense of responsibility when witnessing endangered animals or nature destroyed by human greed, then you already have the heart of a sage. If you see someone struggling and your heart goes out to them, and you want to help, that's evidence of an awakening of the divine within you. Your ability to feel the world's pain as your own and act to heal it reflects the awakening of your benevolent nature.

Sagehood does not require great spiritual powers or dramatic epiphanies. It starts simply with a desire for a peaceful world, happiness for all, and the restoration of the planet. The key is turning that desire into action. Everyone can begin with something small, something achievable today. A small act of kindness, a warm word of encouragement, an effort to care for others, or everyday practices like conserving energy and reducing waste are all expressions of sagehood. In this sense, living as a sage is much like being a conscientious and responsible community member.

Humans are often described as being half-animal and half-divine. While we have natural instincts and impulses for survival, these alone rarely satisfy us because the divine within us craves something more. Animals are content as long as their basic needs are met, but humans can feel a profound emptiness, even when surrounded by the finest foods if their inner sense of meaning and purpose is unfulfilled. This is because, at our core, we are spiritual beings who inherently seek connection, meaning, and purpose.

Our brains are equipped with a survival mode that prioritizes self-interest, but they also have a sagehood mode that activates our conscience, empathy, and benevolent nature. Which mode we operate in is not fixed; it's a choice we make in each moment. Just as a light bulb must be turned on to illuminate and a bell must be struck to chime, sagehood mode requires conscious effort to activate. When we choose to act with love, empathy, and care—no matter how small the gesture—we are already embodying the mindset of a sage.

The Call to Sagehood

The next decade may be one of the most transformative periods in human history. Climate change, advances in AI, political and economic unrest, biodiversity loss, and resource depletion are challenges pressing on us all at once. These issues demand attention and action from everyone. We can no longer afford to stand back and simply observe. While we cannot predict exactly how these changes will unfold, one thing is certain: their consequences will impact not only our lives but also future generations, all life on Earth, and the planet as a whole.

Our brains have immense creativity and potential. This power has brought every advance in knowledge, technology, art, and culture. The achievements of civilization and the richness of life we enjoy today are products of its capabilities. Yet, we are not using our brains to their fullest potential. Our collective consciousness has yet to mature enough to consistently prioritize the planet's well-being over individual or group interests. Instead, we have often used the brain's incredible power to create problems like environmental destruction, social inequality, and war.

Earth is the only habitable planet we know of—a miraculous ecosystem that has sustained life for billions of years. It is home to countless species, not just humans. Yet, we are damaging this precious home, sometimes out of indifference and sometimes in the pursuit of convenience and profit.

Our brains were not designed only to compete, dominate, or destroy. They can build a better world through empathy, connection, and collaboration. It is a tragic misuse of our potential when we allow this extraordinary brainpower to harm each other and our planet.

History shows us that humanity has always found strength and creativity in times of crisis. We have overcome pandemics, achieved technological breakthroughs, and expanded freedom and human rights. These achievements demonstrate what we are capable of. Yet, what we have accomplished so far may only scratch the surface of our potential. We cannot only solve today's challenges but can envision and create new ways of living and being that have never existed before.

Moreover, we are living in the most connected era in human history. Events on the other side of the world can affect us in real time, and one individual's voice can reach a global audience. Thanks to the internet and technological advancements, we now have unparalleled opportunities to collaborate across physical and cultural boundaries. In the past, the power to shape the world was concentrated in the hands of kings, leaders, and a small elite. Today, ordinary people have more power than ever to drive change.

Many are now recognizing global issues, speaking out, and taking action. Instead of simply worrying about the state of the world, they are finding ways to contribute and act on them. What was once expected of only a few visionaries or sages is now becoming part of the mindset of ordinary people. This shift represents an expansion of our collective consciousness and an awakening of our spirituality and shared sense of responsibility.

However, there is no guarantee that this unique opportunity will last. This may be the first—and possibly the last—time humanity has the chance to collectively address these challenges. We've seen with our own eyes and felt with our bodies the crises facing humanity and the planet. We know the root causes of these problems and have the knowledge and technology to address them. Most importantly, we can choose and act, guided by our brains and minds.

This is a time when we are all called to embrace sagehood—not as a pursuit of perfection, but as a commitment to compassion, responsibility, and meaningful action. The planet doesn't need just one or two sages; it needs thousands, even millions. When each of us draws upon the wisdom, empathy, and accountability within ourselves, we have the power to create a culture on Earth unlike anything we have ever known.

When we embrace the heart of a sage, we can use the power of our brains to move beyond patterns of competition and destruction and build a culture of cooperation and mutual support. Instead of rejecting differences, we can learn from one another and find inspiration in our diversity. Rather than exploiting the planet's resources, we can focus on restoring and protecting the environment. And, instead of chasing material gain alone, we can seek a balance between the material and the spiritual, creating a world where the depth and beauty of life are nurtured and sustained.

A World Where Everyone Is a Sage

One day, while listening to the song *The Leopard of Kilimanjaro* by the Korean singer Cho Yong-pil, I was struck by the lyrics: "I am in this world now because the 21st century wanted me so badly." It felt like a profound declaration of purpose. If I am here because the 21st century needs me, then I have a responsibility to contribute to the world in a meaningful way. Even if my presence makes the world just a little brighter or more positive, that's enough to make my life feel meaningful and worthwhile.

None of us chose to come into this world, yet we are all here, navigating life and searching for purpose. There is no predetermined role or purpose handed to us. But when we realize our innate divinity and recognize our true worth by activating our BrainPhone, we can define our purpose and live with intention. While being born was beyond our control, discovering our value and setting a direction for our lives empowers us to take control of our destiny.

Each and every one of us has the right to declare: "I am in this world now because the 21st century wanted me so badly!" Our essence is rooted in divinity and eternal life. To say that I am here, in this moment, because the universe deeply wants me to be, is not an exaggeration. It's a truth and a powerful reminder of the profound value and significance each of us carries.

When we recognize our own worth, we can develop self-respect, trust, and faith in ourselves. This awareness drives us to live in alignment with the high values and principles we choose for ourselves. It also enables us to respect one another and build true solidarity and empathy, understanding that we all share the same fundamental worth.

Still, many of us underestimate ourselves. We question whether we matter in a world so vast or whether we can make a meaningful difference when we can't always control our own lives. This doubt is a mistake. Every one of us has a brain, a mind, and the innate capacity to shape our lives. When we extend that capacity outward, even in small ways, we can help create a more sustainable and peaceful world.

We must never, under any circumstance, diminish our own worth. We must never undervalue humanity or lose hope and faith in ourselves or others. No matter how challenging life may seem, the strength to overcome those challenges lies within us. While many of humanity's problems are man-made, the solutions lie within us too. We are not only our hope; we are humanity's hope.

The power to heal our minds and bodies and to create a sustainable and peaceful world does not come from advanced technology or large investments. It resides in the minds and hearts of a sage. Often, it's the smallest actions that make the most significant difference. Love and empathy cannot be manufactured or calculated; they are uniquely human traits. We, as sages, are called to offer the world these.

Declare Yourself a Sage

When you feel like giving up on your dreams or when hope is slipping away, pause to reset and reawaken your spirit. Try a Brain Sport activity—any activity that energizes you and connects you with your inner strength. Then, turn on your BrainPhone and declare with conviction:

"I'm going to do this!"
"I am here because the 21st century needs me!"
"I am my own hope and the hope of the world!"
"I am a sage!"

At first, it might feel awkward or even silly. You might laugh at yourself or feel unsure. But go ahead and say it out loud anyway. Stand tall, puff out your chest, and speak boldly and confidently. As you do, you'll feel a deep resonance within you. Your brain will recognize the power of your words, absorb their meaning, and begin to embrace them.

Our brains are naturally attuned to the power of words and tend to act in alignment with what we repeatedly affirm. The more you reinforce this declaration, the more your brain will engage its neuroplasticity to bring it to life. It will draw on all its resources—imagination, creativity, persistence, and determination—to support you in living as a sage and fulfilling your potential.

By engaging in Brain Sports, you train your mind and body to work in harmony and turn on your BrainPhone, strengthening your connection to your inner wisdom. This process helps you align your actions with your highest values and step into the role of a sage in every moment.

Even in everyday tasks, such as cooking a meal or doing a single pull-up, approach them as sage actions. Imagine each task as something the 21st-century world needs from you. No matter how small the action, seeing it in this manner gives it greater meaning. Make it a Brain Sport in this way, and you'll approach it with more care, passion, and thoughtfulness.

You don't need to carry the weight of the world to make a difference. You can contribute to the life and world you envision with a positive mindset, playful energy, and a confident attitude. Sagehood isn't rooted in being overly serious—it lies in finding joy and strength in the actions you take and letting that joy empower you to do more. I encourage that joy when I motivate others to try pull-ups and teach them how to do it. It especially comes out when someone attempts their first pull-up. They often exclaim, "I did it!" or "I can't believe I did it!" Watching people push beyond their perceived limits and uncover their inner strength is truly inspiring and heartening.

When someone overcomes the belief of "I can't do it" through pull-ups, they build the confidence to tackle other challenges in their life. They come to realize that persistence and effort can help them achieve more than they ever imagined. That hope and belief don't just benefit them—it spreads to others and contributes to the greater good. I often say, half-jokingly but with real conviction, "Brain pull-ups are the best exercise for stepping into sagehood."

Any action, no matter how small, that benefits yourself and the world is an act of sagehood. Through these actions, both big and small, we can express the heart of a sage in every area of our lives. We can also inspire and encourage this spirit in one another, building a shared commitment to positive change.

When all our efforts come together, sagehood will no longer be seen as something rare or extraordinary—it will become a shared way of living, rooted in common sense. In a world where everyone strives to embody this wisdom, humanity can take a meaningful step toward a new spiritual era, one where we collectively realize our highest potential. And that journey can start today, with something as simple as taking on one pull-up.

CLOSING THOUGHTS

SEEING BEYOND REALITY

When our minds are trapped in the memories of the past and the reality in front of us, it can feel impossible to overcome limitations and obstacles. It may seem like a pipe dream for humanity to move beyond a materialistic, competition-driven life and create a world that prioritizes spiritual growth and a culture of coexistence.

But if we turn on the BrainPhone and reconnect with our brains, we open a new eye to see beyond reality. We rediscover our forgotten greatness and realize that our essence is divine, vibrating with infinite wisdom, creativity, and possibility. In that moment, we can dream again, imagine beyond the constraints of past experiences and current reality, and take concrete steps to bring those dreams to life.

A dream is a reality that has not yet come true. But when we become the masters of our brains, we can vividly feel that our dreams are already realized in our minds. Even if they seem distant in the physical world, within our minds, we can see them clearly and move toward them with purpose. That will and hope become guiding lights that illuminate our path.

Turn on your BrainPhone and connect with the mind of a sage within you through feelings, not thoughts. Strengthen and nurture that mind through Brain Sports activities. That connection will give you the confidence to overcome the limitations of reality and open new paths forward.

The most beautiful thing we can do with the great mind we have taken back is to practice unconditional love. Respect and love yourself unconditionally, and treat all life with care and compassion. I am deeply grateful to those who are already inspiring others by living such a life. Let's make the world more beautiful and brighter through the power of our great minds and hearts.

ACKNOWLEDGMENTS

I am deeply grateful to everyone who contributed their time, talent, and care to bring this book to life. Their support has been a constant source of encouragement throughout this journey.

Steve Kim provided invaluable insights that enriched the content and sharpened its focus. Jiyoung Oh, Michela Mangiaracina, and Nicole Dean ensured the manuscript was clear and polished through their skilled editing. Kiryl Lysenka gave the book structure and character with his thoughtful design.

I also appreciate the feedback from Sohyung Lim, David Driscoll, and Haerang Ihm, which helped refine the ideas and improve accessibility.

To everyone who supported this work, thank you for your encouragement, belief in its message, and vision for a better world. This book reflects your generosity and care.

RESOURCES

Body & Brain Yoga and Tai Chi Centers

Body & Brain Yoga Tai Chi centers offer classes in yoga, tai chi, qigong, and meditation based on Ilchi Lee's Brain Education and energy principles. There are about 70 centers across the U.S. with more in South Korea, Japan, Europe, Canada, and New Zealand. Group classes, workshops, and individual sessions are available both in person and online. Find a U.S. center near you at BodynBrain.com.

Ilchi Lee's Email Newsletter

Ilchi Lee shares a weekly newsletter that provides insights into personal development, mindful living, and adopting an earth-citizen lifestyle. It includes practical advice, meditation techniques, and ideas for contributing to a more peaceful and sustainable world. To subscribe, visit ilchi.com/newsletter.

Brain Education TV on YouTube

Brain Education TV provides practical videos with brain tips, meditations, and exercises to support your well-being and boost brain function. The channel shares inspiring stories and simple practices to help you build self-confidence, improve focus, and live with greater health and happiness. Subscribe at youtube.com/BrainEducationTV.

BOOKS OF RELATED INTEREST

The following books by Ilchi Lee help you unlock your brain's potential and live a more authentic, fulfilling life. Explore these titles and more at BestLifeMedia.com.

The Power Brain

Five Steps
to Upgrading Your Brain
Operating System

I've Decided to Live 120 Years

The Ancient Secret to Longevity,
Vitality, and Life Transformation

The Art of Coexistence

How You and I
Can Save the World

A New Humanity

Embracing Our
Responsibility for the Earth

NOTES

CHAPTER 1: WHEN MACHINES STEAL OUR MINDS

1. "Stress in Modern Britain," The Psychological Society (2017), https://www.physoc.org/policy/stress-in-modern-britain.
2. Gloria Mark, *Attention Span: A Groundbreaking Way to Restore Balance, Happiness, and Productivity, (*Toronto: Hanover Square Press, 2023).
3. "Brain Rot Named Oxford Word of the Year 2024," Oxford University Press, December 2, 2024, https://corp.oup.com/news/brain-rot-named-oxford-word-of-the-year.
4. Laurie A. Manwell et al., "Digital Dementia in the Internet Generation: Excessive Screen Time During Brain Development Will Increase the Risk of Alzheimer's Disease and Related Dementias in Adulthood," *Journal of Integrative Neuroscience* 21, no. 1 (2022): 28, https://pubmed.ncbi.nlm.nih.gov/35164464.
5. Matt Stefl and Andrew Rohm, "Is the Internet Killing Your Creative Potential?" *Graziadio Business Review,* 20(1), https://digitalcommons.lmu.edu/cgi/viewcontent.cgi?article=1005&context=mbl_fac.
6. Yang-Yang Li et al., "Internet Addiction Increases in the General Population During COVID-19: Evidence From China," https://pmc.ncbi.nlm.nih.gov/articles/PMC8251395.
7. Jonathan Haidt, *The Anxious Generation: How the Great Rewiring of Childhood Is Causing an Epidemic of Mental Illness,* (New York: Penguin Press, 2024).
8. Georgia Wells et al., "Facebook Knows Instagram Is Toxic for Teen Girls, Company Documents Show," *The Wall Street Journal,* September 14, 2021, https://www.wsj.com/articles/facebook-knows-instagram-is-toxic-for-teen-girls-company-documents-show-11631620739.

CHAPTER 2: TURN ON YOUR BRAINPHONE

1. Will Henshall, "When Might AI Outsmart Us? It Depends Who You Ask," *Time*, January 19, 2024, https://time.com/6556168/when-ai-outsmart-humans.
2. Anthony Cuthbertson, "AI Poses Risks on Par with Nuclear Weapons, Experts Warn," *The Independent*, May 31, 2023, https://www.independent.co.uk/tech/ai-existential-risk-deepmind-openai-b2348380.html.

CHAPTER 3: LIFE IS A GAME OF BRAIN SPORTS

1. Jesus Ilundain-Agurruza and Mizuho Takemura, "Philosophy of Sport: Eastern Philosophy and Pragmatism," Academia.edu, https://www.academia.edu/15167100/Philosophy_of_Sport_Eastern_Philosophy_and_Pragmatism.

CHAPTER 4: ALIGN YOUR INNER VIBRATION

1. Jesang Park, *Budoji,* edited and translated by Eunsu Kim, (Seoul: Hanmunhwa Multimedia, 2012).
2. "Tacoma Narrows Bridge: Lessons from the Failure of a Great Machine," Washington State Department of Transportation, https://wsdot.wa.gov/TNBhistory/bridges-failure.htm.
3. "Broughton Suspension Bridge," Wikimedia Foundation, last modified November 12, 2023, https://en.wikipedia.org/wiki/Broughton_Suspension_Bridge.

CHAPTER 5: ENERGIZE YOUR IMAGINATION

1. Brian C. Clark et al., "The Power of the Mind: the Cortex as a Critical Determinant of Muscle Strength/Weakness," *Journal of Neurophysiology* 112, no. 12 (2014), https://journals.physiology.org/doi/pdf/10.1152/jn.00386.2014.
2. Ellen J. Langer, *Counterclockwise: Mindful Health and the Power of Possibility*, (New York: Ballantine Books, 2009).

3. Riki Lindsay et al., "The Effect of Mental Imagery on Skill Performance in Sport: A Systematic Review," *Journal of Science and Medicine in Sport* 22 (2019), https://www.jsams.org/article/S1440-2440(19)31014-X/abstract.
4. Donatella Di Corrado et al., "Mental Imagery Skills in Competitive Young Athletes and Non-athletes," *Frontiers in Psychology* 11 (2020), https://www.frontiersin.org/journals/psychology/articles/10.3389/fpsyg.2020.00633.

CHAPTER 6: RECLAIM YOUR CREATIVITY

1. Antonio Damasio, *Descartes' Error: Emotion, Reason, and the Human Brain,* (New York: Putnam Publishing, 1994).
2. Owen Giddens and Sandra Giddens, *Chinese Mythology,* (New York, Rosen Publishing Group, 2006).
3. Angela L. Duckworth et al., "Grit: Perseverance and Passion for Long-Term Goals," *Journal of Personality and Social Psychology* 92, no. 6 (2007), https://www.researchgate.net/publication/6290064.

CHAPTER 8: EXERCISE TO TRANSFORM YOUR LIFE

1. Julie Corliss, "How Much Do You Sit, Stand, and Move Each Day?" Harvard Health Publishing, last modified November 10, 2023, https://www.health.harvard.edu/heart-health/how-much-do-you-sit-stand-and-move-each-day.
2. "Sitting Disease: How a Sedentary Lifestyle Affects Heart Health," Johns Hopkins Medicine, https://www.hopkinsmedicine.org/health/wellness-and-prevention/sitting-disease-how-a-sedentary-lifestyle-affects-heart-health.
3. James A. Levine, "Sick of Sitting," *Diabetologia* 58, no. 8 (2015), https://mayoclinic.elsevierpure.com/en/publications/sick-of-sitting.
4. Jeremy Sibold and Kathy Berg, "Mood Enhancement Persists for up to 12 Hours Following Aerobic Exercise: a Pilot Study," *Perceptual and Motor Skills* 111, no 2 (2010), https://europepmc.org/article/MED/21162437.

5. "Lower Risk of Depression with Elevated Exercise," *The Harvard Gazette,* November 5, 2019, https://news.harvard.edu/gazette/story/2019/11/physical-activity-may-protect-those-at-risk-for-depression.
6. Ben Singh et al., "Effectiveness of Physical Activity Interventions for Improving Depression, Anxiety and Distress: An Overview of Systematic Reviews," *British Journal of Sports Medicine* 57, no. 18 (2023), https://bjsm.bmj.com/content/57/18/1203.
7. Kirk I. Erickson et al., "Exercise Training Increases Size of Hippocampus and Improves Memory," *Proceedings of the National Academy of Sciences* 108, no. 7 (2011): 3017–3022, https://www.jstor.org/stable/41002254.
8. Julia C. Basso et al., "Acute Exercise Improves Prefrontal Cortex but Not Hippocampal Function in Healthy Adults," *Journal of the International Neuropsychological Society* 21, no. 10 (2015), https://pubmed.ncbi.nlm.nih.gov/26581791.
9. Monèm Jemni et al., "Exercise Improves Depression Through Positive Modulation of Brain-Derived Neurotrophic Factor (BDNF): A Review Based on 100 Manuscripts Over 20 Years," *Frontiers in Physiology* 14 (2023), https://www.frontiersin.org/journals/physiology/articles/10.3389/fphys.2023.1102526.
10. Kathleen A. Martin Ginis et al., "Formulation of Evidence-Based Messages to Promote the Use of Physical Activity to Prevent and Manage Alzheimer's Disease," *BMC Public Health* 17, Article 209 (2017), https://bmcpublichealth.biomedcentral.com/articles/10.1186/s12889-017-4090-5.
11. Marily Oppezzo and Daniel L. Schwartz, "Give Your Ideas Some Legs: The Positive Effect of Walking on Creative Thinking," *Journal of Experimental Psychology: Learning, Memory, and Cognition* 40, no. 4 (2014), https://www.apa.org/pubs/journals/releases/xlm-a0036577.pdf.
12. Christian Rominger et. al., "Habitual physical activity is related to more creative activities and achievements," *Scientific Reports* 14, 29768 (2024), https://www.nature.com/articles/s41598-024-80714-6.

CHAPTER 9: MEDITATE TO STAY AWAKE

1. Eileen Luders et al., "The Underlying Anatomical Correlates of Long-Term Meditation: Larger Hippocampal and Frontal Volumes of Gray Matter," *NeuroImage* 45, no. 3 (2009): 672–678, https://doi.org/10.1016/j.neuroimage.2008.12.061.
2. Gaëlle Desbordes et al., "Effects of Mindful-Attention and Compassion Meditation Training on Amygdala Response to Emotional Stimuli in an Ordinary, Non-Meditative State," *Frontiers in Human Neuroscience* 6 (2012): 292, https://doi.org/10.3389/fnhum.2012.00292.
3. Yi-Yuan Tang et al. "Short-Term Meditation Training Improves Attention and Self-Regulation," *Proceedings of the National Academy of Sciences* 104, no. 43 (2007): 17152–17156, https://doi.org/10.1073/pnas.0707678104.
4. Sara Lazar et al., "Meditation experience is associated with increased cortical thickness," *NeuroReport* 16, no. 17 (2005): 1893–1897, https://doi.org/10.1097/01.wnr.0000186598.66243.19.
5. "Hair Analysis Shows: Meditation Training Reduces Long-Term Stress," Max Planck Institute for Human Cognitive and Brain Sciences, October 7, 2021, https://maxplanckneuroscience.org/hair-analysis-shows-meditation-training-reduces-long-term-stress.
6. Fadel Zeidan et al., "Mindfulness Meditation Improves Cognition: Evidence of Brief Mental Training," *Consciousness and Cognition* 19, no. 2 (2010): 597–605, https://doi.org/10.1016/j.concog.2010.03.014.
7. Elizabeth Hoge et al., "Loving-Kindness Meditation Practice Associated with Longer Telomeres in Women," *Brain, Behavior, and Immunity* 32 (2013): 159–163, https://doi.org/10.1016/j.bbi.2013.04.005.
8. Judson Brewer et al., "Meditation Experience Is Associated with Differences in Default Mode Network Activity and Connectivity," *Proceedings of the National Academy of Sciences* 108, no. 50 (2011), https://doi.org/10.1073/pnas.1112029108.

9. Deborah Bowden et al., "A Comparative Randomised Controlled Trial of the Effects of Brain Wave Vibration Training, Iyengar Yoga, and Mindfulness on Mood, Well-Being, and Salivary Cortisol," *Evidence-Based Complementary and Alternative Medicine* (2012), https://doi.org/10.1155/2012/234713.

CHAPTER 10: BE POSITIVE AND GRATEFUL

1. Barbara L. Fredrickson, "The Role of Positive Emotions in Positive Psychology: The Broaden-and-Build Theory of Positive Emotions," *American Psychologist* 56, no. 3 (2001), https://www.prospectivepsych.org/sites/default/files/pictures/Frederickson_Broaden-and-build-2001.pdf.
2. Lisa R. Yanek et al., "Effect of Positive Well-Being on Incidence of Symptomatic Coronary Artery Disease," *The American Journal of Cardiology* 112, Issue B (2013), https://www.ajconline.org/article/S0002-9149(13)01280-0/abstract.

CHAPTER 11: MEET THE DIVINE IN THE BRAIN

1. Anonymous, Ancient Korean text, edited by Hanmunhwa editorial, *Chun Ji In: Chun Bu Kyung, Samil Shingo, Cham Jeon Gye Kyung*, (Seoul: Hanmunhwa Multimedia, 2016).

CHAPTER 12: A WORLD OF EVERYDAY SAGES

1. Merav Weiss-Sidi and Hila Riemer, "Help Others—Be Happy? The Effect of Altruistic Behavior on Happiness Across Cultures," *Frontiers in Psychology*, Volume 14 (2023), https://www.frontiersin.org/journals/psychology/articles/10.3389/fpsyg.2023.1156661.

ABOUT THE AUTHOR

Ilchi Lee is a visionary educator and meditation expert dedicated to teaching energy principles and unlocking the brain's full potential. For over four decades, he has developed and taught mind-body training methods such as Body & Brain Yoga and Brain Education, empowering people world- wide to live healthier, happier lives.

He founded Global Cyber University and the University of Brain Education and has authored over 40 books, including the *New York Times* bestseller *The Call of Sedona: Journey of the Heart*, as well as *The Power Brain: Five Steps to Upgrading Your Brain Operating System* and *I've Decided to Live 120 Years: The Ancient Secret to Longevity, Vitality, and Life Transformation.*

A respected humanitarian, Ilchi Lee has collaborated with the United Nations and other organizations for global peace through the International Brain Education Association (IBREA). He also established the Earth Citizen Movement and the nonprofit Earth Citizens Organization to promote mindful and sustainable living.

For more information, visit Ilchi.com.

9 781947 502338